Art & Design

Roy Jarratt

Series consultant: Chris Drage

Published in 2003 by:
Nelson Thornes Ltd
Delta Place
27 Bath Road
CHELTENHAM
GL53 7TH
United Kingdom

03 04 05 06 07 / 10 9 8 7 6 5 4 3 2 1

A catalogue record for this book is available from the British Library

ISBN 0 7487 7037 2

Page make-up by AMR Ltd

Printed and bound in Spain by GraphyCems

Contents ▼

New curriculum developments have placed Information and Communication Technology (ICT) as a pivotal element of learning across all subject areas. Each subject Programme of Study states that teachers should 'make appropriate use of ICT' within the subject area, and this also includes Art. Further support for starting points is given in the QCA Schemes of Work for each subject. Scottish Guidelines also provide ideas for the integrated use of ICT within the arts and environmental studies.

However, ICT can be little more than a collection of tools for retrieving, creating and processing information unless it is placed within a context. The creative process taught in the Art Scheme of Work, when allied to the tools available on computer, provides not only a wide variety of contexts, but also a way of using the computer to develop creative solutions to problems given, and a clear development in thinking skills.

▼ Why use ICT in Art and Design?

It is important to state at the outset that ICT is not a replacement for observational drawing with pencil, pastel or brush. One of the more advanced techniques, and one which is taught at a later stage, is that of 'drawing' with the computer. It is very difficult to do this with a mouse, and only marginally easier with a pen pad. It is also not the most effective function of a paint package for use with primary pupils. Art-orientated software can help enormously with pupils' understanding of tones and tints, for example by experimenting with the colour wheel, but it can never be a replacement for mixing colour by hand, and should not be thought of as such.

It is, therefore, important to ask what a paint, drawing or image-editing package can offer to teachers and pupils in the primary school.

ICT can make some art processes more efficient, for example exploring a series of pattern repeats of part of an observational drawing. The computer allows pupils to experiment and to try out different combinations of their drawings which will then further their pattern work. In this way, the computer becomes an integral part of the creative process, another tool for pupils to use. The computer may also make possible a more in-depth study of collage techniques, where pupils may move different elements quickly and easily and be able to judge, compare and consider the different effects they achieve.

Many schools now have their own website, and can use this facility to create galleries of completed artwork for other schools to view and comment on. Pupils can also e-mail artwork for comment by a partner school. By the end of KS2/P4–7, pupils are exploring their own designs for web pages, and reapplying skills in composition, use of colour, shape and texture in this new domain.

Once pupils have grasped the idea that the computer is an additional tool for creative artwork, and not a replacement for pencil or brush, they and their teachers will begin to see the possibilities of the use of paint software. The activities in this handbook are designed to aid that development.

To summarise, the ICT Programme of Study and the Programme of Study for Art integrate in the following ways:

ICT	ART
Finding things out • gather information; • enter and store information; • retrieve information that has been stored.	**Exploring and developing ideas** • collect visual information to help develop ideas.
Developing ideas and making things happen • develop and refine ideas by bringing together, organising and reorganising images and sound.	**Investigating and making** • apply experience of materials and processes, developing control of tools and techniques.
Exchanging and sharing information • share and exchange information in a variety of forms, including e-mail; • sensitivity to needs of audience.	**Investigating and making** • use a variety of methods and approaches to communicate observations, ideas and feelings.
Reviewing, modifying and evaluating work as it progresses • review what they have done to help them develop their ideas; • describe the effects of their actions; • talk about what they might change in future work.	**Evaluating and developing work** • compare ideas, methods and approaches in own and others' work and say what they think and feel about them; • adapt their work according to their views and describe how to develop it further.
Breadth of study • work with a range of information to consider its characteristics and purposes; • work with others to explore a variety of information sources and ICT tools.	**Breadth of study** • explore a range of starting points for practical work; • use a range of processes and materials, including ICT; • investigate art, craft and design in the locality and in a variety of genres, styles and traditions.

The above table may be used by the Art co-ordinator and ICT co-ordinator as a basis for joint planning. The activities in this handbook are designed to make the most use of the links given above, and are based on QCA schemes for both subjects, so that pupils learn skills relevant to their year in ICT and apply those same skills in their Art projects.

▼ National Curriculum 2000

Some of the most notable changes in the presentation of the National Curriculum for England that occurred in 2000 included a statement of general teaching requirements, applicable to all subject areas, and with particular importance for the creative subjects, notably Art and Music.

These were organised under the following headings:

- inclusion: providing effective learning opportunities for all pupils, across all subjects;
- six key skills across the curriculum: communication, number, information technology, working with others, improving own learning and performance and problem-solving;
- five areas of thinking skills – knowing how to learn as well as what to learn: information processing, reasoning, enquiry, creative thinking and evaluation.

The issue of access to a clear programme of learning of skills and techniques in Art remains an important one, in particular in relation to those key and core skills described above. Teachers can no longer expect pupils to produce more developed artwork as they grow older, simply because they repeatedly create paintings. As in every other subject, pupils need tools to be able to develop their artwork.

The QCA offers a balanced programme of learning in all aspects of Art, in 2-D and 3-D and using a wide range of materials. There are also several references to the possible uses of ICT to support learning.

However, in addition to these specific references given in the QCA Scheme of Work, teachers now have the opportunity to develop key skills and thinking skills within Art, using ICT as an integral part of the learning process. The projects given for each year are designed to aid that process and provide a meaningful use of ICT within the Art Programme of Study.

Ofsted reports note an increased proportion of schools using the computer for research into the work of a range of artists and craftspeople. More schools make use of DTP software to produce leaflets and a range of greetings cards,

for example, so that pupils have the opportunity to blend text and images and look at basic page layout design. Pupils are more aware of the existence of supporting materials in the form of clip art or scanned images using a digital camera.

However, several issues still face teachers before development of ICT as a subject in its own right, and ICT within other subject areas, can be moved forward:

- ICT work is not always challenging enough;
- there is a lack of time for the ICT co-ordinator to work with the Art co-ordinator to assess pupils' capabilities and the staff's professional needs;
- teachers do not always have time to research appropriate Art-related software;
- there is a lack of projects which support drawing and painting and the key skills in Art, and a gradual progression of those skills as pupils move through each key stage.

To improve the situation, three conditions are necessary.

- The first is equipment, both hardware and software. Many school are providing whole-class learning through computer suites. Classroom provision is varied. Some schools have opted to place their most efficient machines for everyday use, while others see this less as a priority and favour the equipment being available on a 'rota' system for specific ICT activities. The school needs to be clear about its plans for developing whole-class IT skills, and its provision for the development of ICT skills in other subjects. Machines still need to be available in class for use in lessons other than IT.
- The second is the provision of software that allows for the effective integration of ICT skills in other subject areas. This relies on a

teacher having time to explore new software, exchange expertise and build on the success of experience.

- The third area is that of co-ordination of ICT, an effective ICT policy which clearly shows the contributions of each subject area, and a staff training programme and support system.

This handbook aims to address some of these issues by:

- providing a series of ICT activities clearly linked to each Art project in each year group;

- offering a development of skills taught in ICT as a part of its own Programme of Study, which are integrated into each project;
- giving ideas for the necessary software;
- providing clear guidelines for the Art and ICT co-ordinators.

The handbook draws on the Programmes of Study, the QCA Schemes of Work for Art and ICT, Early Learning Goals for the Foundation Stage, the National Curriculum for England and experience of teaching Art/ICT in school to a range of age groups.

Classroom Organisation ▼

There are a number of management issues that relate to the successful use of ICT equipment, particularly the use of the classroom computer. Good classroom organisation contributes greatly to success with the computer and also helps to minimise technical problems.

For some teachers the organisation of the computer into the everyday routine of the classroom presents many difficulties, not least of which is the simple fact that, more often than not, there is only one computer. Teachers may say they do not use the computer for the following reasons:

- it is disruptive;
- they want programs that the pupils can use without a teacher (the computer is regarded as a teaching machine for drill and practice);
- there is no time for the computer;
- time spent on other subjects is more important.

The computer may be regarded as just something that has to be planned for, and for many a reluctant user it can be a real problem. It is easy for all to understand that the computer should be used – indeed the ICT National Curriculum demands that all pupils have access to this technology – but for some the computer is an intimidating piece of machinery. Without the appropriate knowledge, these teachers may well be convinced that the computer and printer never function correctly when they use them.

The following organisational strategies may be worth considering when teachers who are less confident with computers are planning for ICT in Art projects, and as general classroom practice:

- Learn how to load, save and print from the program.
- Initially plan for small, manageable activities.

- Initially identify small group activities in preference to whole-class sessions.
- Limit the amount of software to just a few programs and get to know these well.
- Install the software onto the hard disk first if possible, keeping copies of the floppy disk or CDs.
- Where appropriate, introduce the program to the whole class to ensure a common understanding and starting point.
- Provide some help cards for the program.
- Use classroom support assistants to assist pupils at the computer.
- Make a few rules for the class about asking for help and giving peer support.
- Plan when the computer will be used and by whom, and how much support will be available.
- Ensure that the computer, printer and chosen program are all working together correctly before the pupils start work.
- Set aside some time to discuss with the pupils what they have done (a whole-class discussion may be a valuable way of developing expertise).
- Encourage pupils to save their work regularly, especially before printing (if the printer does not work it may cause the computer to freeze, and the only way to unfreeze the computer is to switch it off, thus losing work).
- Ensure that pupils are clear about the task they are engaging in. Use the introduction to the activities to prepare for interacting with each program. Prepare instruction sheets that can be laminated and displayed by the computer.

As pupils become more confident they can be encouraged to share their expertise with other pupils in the class. This will include starting and quitting programs, saving and printing their work and setting up and putting away

peripherals such as scanners or digital cameras. Some pupils will need extra time and support in developing their skills as independent computer users.

▼ Grouping the pupils

Two pupils can comfortably work at a computer sharing a task such as writing, drawing or painting programs. Three pupils in a group working at the computer is appropriate for projects using a scanner or creating a montage, allowing for each pupil to take a separate role and rotating responsibilities. It is important to ensure that all the pupils are sharing the activity, and the tasks should be rotated to ensure that one or two pupils do not dominate.

▼ Positioning the computer

The siting of the computer is of immediate importance. Most classrooms were built before the computer was invented, and they are frequently not ideal places for computer use. Some considerations follow:

- It is best to make the position as permanent as security will permit, keeping the computer system as far away from the chalkboard as possible.
- Ideally, the computer should be placed away from bright light to avoid reflection on the screen. Reflections not only make the screen difficult to read, but also detract from concentration on the work at hand.
- Similarly, it is important that the screen does not face the rest of the class; pupils working at the computer do not then feel that they must protect their work from onlookers and nor, in turn, are the rest of the class distracted.
- Having the computer near the carpet helps when introducing a new program to the

whole class, giving them somewhere comfortable to sit as a group.
- Although it is tempting to enclose the computer table with bookshelves and screens, adequate space must be retained for pupils to sit comfortably and for their sketchbooks, help cards and other materials. Restricting the space around the computer also makes it very awkward to reload the printer with paper or to do any other technical checking.
- All mains cables should be placed out of the way and it is advisable to use a multi-point socket with its own on/off switch. If you can afford one that isolates the system from the effects of power surge, so much the better. It is wiser to provide sockets for future peripherals such as a control interface or overlay keyboard.
- EC Directives on computer use, coupled with the problems that can arise in accommodating new systems, highlight many shortcomings and compromises across the school that the acquisition of modern furniture would help eliminate. In a primary school it is important to site the stand-alone machine correctly so that the best use can be made of it.
- As computer use frequently means a group activity, enough space must be available for a group of three pupils to sit comfortably around the screen. Younger pupils are far more likely to need extra space for an overlay keyboard, whilst older pupils may need space for a scanner and a range of source materials.
- In primary schools a computer is often a shared resource or must be moved around the teaching/learning area. A trolley should be chosen with rubber wheels at least 75 mm in diameter, two of which incorporate brakes. The trolley should be able to fit through a standard 650 mm doorway but

also conform to the 800 mm depth necessary to comply with the EC VDU directive. To meet these two demands, the worktop must slide out to its working position and be able to retract safely before being moved. For stand-alone systems like multimedia computers in a library or learning resource area, large mobile trolley workstations are more appropriate.

Standard computer furniture would not be appropriate for wheelchair or standing frame users. The answer here is to provide a suitable type of adjustable furniture that can cope with infinite variations in height. Similarly, with the visually impaired or those who have restricted mobility and co-ordination, a variety of input devices may be needed (e.g. switches, overlay keyboard, tracker ball). A larger workstation is called for to accommodate these extra items safely.

No matter where or whom you teach, there must be an agreed, co-ordinated action plan for ICT so that new computer systems, peripherals and furniture all combine successfully.

▼ Time management

The management of time poses the biggest problem by far. It is vital that the teacher is familiar with the software and hardware and time must be given to do this. This is important so that the teacher may make an estimate of how long each group might need to complete a task. The amount of time a group needs at the computer really depends on the type of software being used. Pupils might need anything from ten minutes to a few hours to complete a piece of work, depending on the type of activity. When using ICT as part of Art activities, pupils will be working in groups using the computer in rotation. This needs careful planning so that pupils do not become impatient waiting for a 'turn' and distract the pupils who are trying to complete their task.

▼ Tasks, roles and responsibilities – the co-ordinator's role

The role and responsibilities of the ICT co-ordinator are increasingly complex. Although there are many 'standard' areas which all schools will expect to be the responsibility of the ICT co-ordinator, there are others which might belong to the senior management team or the Art co-ordinator. Detailed guidance on the role of the ICT co-ordinator in developing and managing ICT in school is given in the *Primary ICT Handbook Science* (Nelson Thornes, 2001). The main issues are highlighted in this handbook to illustrate where responsibilities merge and where each co-ordinator has a discrete role.

One of the first tasks a new ICT co-ordinator will embark on is writing and amending the ICT policy. As with all policy documents this will be carried out in collaboration with the subject co-ordinators and will have a twofold purpose and audience. For members of the school staff the ICT policy is an important document in ensuring that an agreed approach is understood and carried out. It will also assist in planning and promote development of ICT.

For parents, the local community, outside agencies and organisations the policy will explain the school's position and support the allocation of funds. It will need to be linked to the School Development Plan and cross-referenced to other documentation such as the National Curriculum, the Early Learning Goals, etc.

▼ Writing an ICT policy

Audit ▼

An audit of existing hardware and software is an essential aspect of writing the policy, as members of staff need to be clear about what is part of ICT. The following can be used as a checklist for general use across the curriculum:

Hardware	Software
Audio and visual recorders	Control
Calculators	CD-ROM resources
Computers	E-mail
Digital cameras	Databases
Electronic musical instruments	Data logging
Inclusive technology, e.g. overlay keyboards	Desktop publishing
Light sensors	Drawing programs
Pressure pads	Internet
Printers	Multimedia
Programmable toys/ devices	Painting programs
Scanners	Spreadsheets
Temperature sensors and probes	Subject specific programs
Voice-operated equipment	Word processors

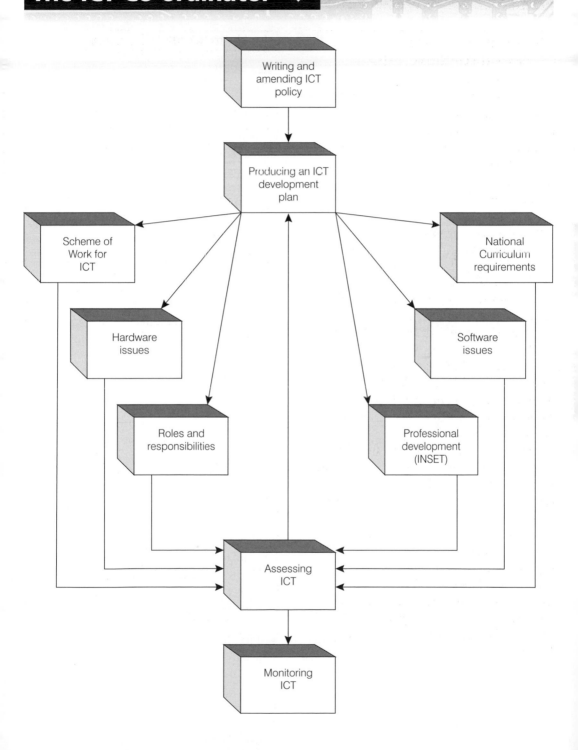

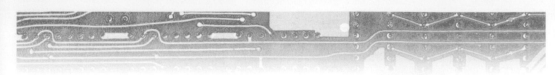

Having audited hardware and software, the ICT co-ordinator will need to take into consideration internal, local and national factors before writing or amending an ICT policy.

- Internal factors will include the school's general aims; the School Development Plan; special features of the school's curriculum; strengths and interests of staff.
- Local factors include the Local Education Authority targets; school partnerships; intake characteristics; support available, e.g. for special needs.
- National factors are the National Curriculum requirements; Ofsted feedback from inspections; national training targets.

Curriculum organisation ▼

In considering the school's curriculum organisation the following questions will need to be asked:

- How will the school deliver the National Curriculum ICT requirements?
- How is ICT capability developed through other subjects?
- Can ICT capability be developed through topic-based work?
- How is differentiation planned?
- How does ICT support and enrich learning across the curriculum?

Teaching and learning styles ▼

The ICT policy will state clearly the roles and responsibilities for key areas of ICT in the school. Learning and teaching styles need to be addressed with a statement of what learning styles can be supported; what teaching styles are encouraged and how differentiation will take place between learners to ensure that each pupil is challenged.

Access to ICT ▼

Access to ICT needs to be stated in the policy document: where equipment is located and used, e.g. class-based computers; computer clusters; networked computers; portable computers; printing facilities; other peripherals such as scanners, cameras, etc.; control and data-logging equipment.

When and how ICT is used will also be stated, for instance, can pupils use the ICT equipment outside lessons? Are pupils able to use ICT equipment unsupervised? Is there a loan scheme for portable equipment? A statement of equal opportunity for pupils to use ICT equipment would address the following questions:

- How do you ensure that all pupils have opportunities to use ICT according to their needs?
- How does ICT help to give pupils with special educational needs access to the whole curriculum?
- How does ICT support more able pupils?
- How do you take account of gender issues?
- How do you take account of pupils' access to ICT at home?

Assessment issues ▼

The ICT policy will address general issues regarding recording, assessment and reporting and indicate the following:

- How the practice with ICT reflects the school's policy on recording, assessment and reporting;
- The additional demands that need to be taken into account;
- The use of a school portfolio of ICT work;
- The agreed format for record-keeping;
- Mechanisms for agreement trialling in ICT;
- How much evidence of individual ICT work is kept and for how long.

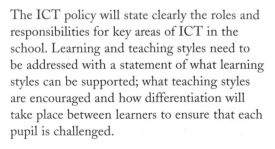

Managing resources ▼

The budget is pivotal in resourcing ICT and will be allocated by a number of different strategies according to the structure and development needs of the school. It may be allocated annually on a formula basis or negotiated each year. A long, medium and short term plan needs to be decided on and included in the ICT policy. Hardware and software, having been audited, need to be kept updated, as do issues of staff training to ensure effective use of ICT resources.

Monitoring and reviewing the policy ▼

Having written or amended an existing policy, the ICT co-ordinator needs to:
- monitor practice to ensure the implementation of the policy through the Schemes of Work;
- monitor staff development;
- set out when the policy will next be reviewed.

The Art co-ordinator will play their part in the overall co-ordination of the ICT provision with a specific brief for the aspects detailed below.

▼ The Art co-ordinator's role

An Art co-ordinator is expected to provide professional leadership that leads to high-quality teaching, effective use of resources and improved standards of achievement. It is vital that the Art co-ordinator ensures that pupils are given opportunities to develop and apply their information technology capability in their Art activities throughout each Key Stage. This requires that:

- ICT is used appropriately to enhance pupils' understanding of the work of a wide range of artists and designers in a range of materials;
- Investigating and making is enhanced by ICT by increasing the range of tools and techniques available to pupils for the study of colour, shape and pattern;
- Pupils are given appropriate opportunities to use ICT to generate and develop their ideas;
- There should be appropriate progression in skills, knowledge and understanding of use of the computer in Art-related activities.

As information and communication technologies develop further, teachers and pupils need opportunities to use these technologies in appropriate ways. For example, teachers should be able to evaluate the potential of video-conferencing, e-mail communication and Internet access as tools for learning. More generally, the school should offer support for teachers' attempts to bring ICT into the Art curriculum. This requires recognition that ICT facilities such as a digital camera and a scanner are as essential as paint, pencil and brush, and that teachers may require additional training in the implementation of ICT in Art.

When writing the Art policy for the school, the co-ordinator needs to clarify with the staff which aspects of ICT relate directly to Art activities, and where links can be made. The table on page 2 shows these links clearly. The use of computers for textiles design and for investigating colour, shape and pattern has already been identified. The activities in this handbook will explore and develop these areas for each year group, and also offer a clear guideline for each project in the Scheme of Work for Art where ICT may be used both to

support the artwork being generated and to reapply the skills pupils have learned in their IT lesson. Scanners can be used as an aid to creating surface pattern designs, as can digital cameras. Scanners are particularly useful in allowing pupils to import their own work in progress, develop it using the tools of a paint program and print the result for further development by hand.

▼ Professional development

To make full use of the opportunities ICT offers to Art education in school, the Art co-ordinator will need to audit existing practice and teacher expertise and review Art Schemes of Work before preparing a

development plan with the ICT co-ordinator. A number of approaches to staff development need to be adopted, again working closely with the ICT co-ordinator. Initially, it is important to establish staff confidence with Art practice and use that as a starting point for developing the ICT activities. It is of vital importance, too, that where staff are not confident with the teaching of drawing and painting skills by hand, they realise that they are not expected to teach pupils to draw using a mouse. It is also important to employ strategies which will develop confidence in skills, whether informal support after school, working alongside colleagues in the classroom or twilight, half- or whole-day in-service training in addition to developing activities for classroom practice.

Resources and ICT Resources Checklist ▼

Most of the activities in this handbook can be carried out with generic software packages. However, it is assumed that the following resources are available:

▼ Hardware resources

It is essential that pupils have access to:
- a computer;
- a printer (preferably colour);
- a digital camera,
- a scanner;
- a multimedia computer;
- the Internet and e-mail.

▼ ICT Resources Checklist

▼ Local area networks

Local area networks (LANs) offer a range of benefits to learning, deployment and management of resources. These are outlined in the Nelson Thornes' *Primary ICT Handbook Science*. Most of the activities in this handbook can be carried out using stand-alone computers and software.

Resource	Activity age	Links to DfES/QCA Art
KS1		
My World (SEMERC)	YR/P1	colour, shape, pattern
Paint software	YR1–2/P1–3	1A, 1B, 2A, 2B, 2D
Digital camera/Scanner	Y2/P3	2A, 2C
Internet	Y1–2/P2–3	1C
KS2		
Desktop publishing	Y3–5/P4–6	5B, 6B
Internet access	Y3–6/P4–7	4B, 5B
CD-ROM resource	Y3–6/P4–7	throughout – clip art, photos
Graphics hardware/software	Y3–6/P4–7	3C, 4C
Painting software	Y3–6/P4–7	3A, 3B, 4A, 5A, 5C, 6C
Multimedia software	Y3–6/P4–7	5A, 6A, 6B

This section lists software from those that are currently available that will support learning in Art. In addition to these, the activities can be adapted to use available programs, e.g. *Microsoft Paint* (Microsoft), *ClarisWorks* or *AppleWorks* (both Apple Computers inc).

▼ Recording using text and pictures

▶ KS 1 / P1–3

 MyWorld 4 (Granada Learning) – PC CD-ROM

This software helps with basic computer skills in clicking and dragging objects on-screen. The screens include, for example, colour-matching, dressing teddy, creating a street scene, number bonding. It is colourful and easy to use. Pupils can also save their work to the *MyWorld* folder.

▶ KS 1–2 / P1–7

Clicker 4 (Crick Software) – Mac/PC

This provides an on-screen keyboard which enables pupils to write with whole words, phrases and pictures. It comes with its own built-in word processor but can also be used alongside other word-processing programs.

 Granada Writer (Granada Learning) – PC CD-ROM

Part of the *Granada Toolkit*. The software allows pupils to import text, pictures, sound and video, and can be used for simple montage effects.

 Talking First Word (Research Machines) – PC

This has four coded levels which introduce the various icons over the pupils' time in school, ranging from simple to the more complex adult version. One program can then be used throughout the school, for all ages of pupils. It also has a speech tool which allows text to be spoken aloud by the computer. This is especially good to assist those pupils who need extra support in literacy.

▼ Painting programs

▶ KS 1 / P1–3

 2paint (2simple Educational Software) – PC CD-ROM

This is a very accessible painting/drawing program designed and developed for YR/P1 pupils where icons representing eight large and eight small felt-tip pens are selected to draw on the screen.

Granada Colours (Granada Learning) – PC CD-ROM

Part of the *Granada Toolkit*, this offers a number of features which allow pupils to draw freehand, use a brush effect, fill, spray, diffuse, clone and stamp. It also has an edit facility.

▶ KS 1–2 / P1–7

 Dazzle Plus (SEMERC) – PC CD-ROM

This is a drawing and painting package that can be configured to add or reduce the number of tools available. It also includes special effects: tiling, rainbow colour cycling, two- and four-way symmetry, and is described as very flexible and easy to use.

 RM Colour Magic (Research Machines) – PC

This has four colour-coded levels which enable the program to be used throughout the pupils' primary years. The basic level is a simple painting package, whereas the most sophisticated level allows pupils to crop images and use special effects. It includes a collection of curriculum-relevant stamps which pupils can use in their work.

▼ Drawing programs

▶ KS 2 / P4–7

 AspexDraw (Aspex Software) – PC CD-ROM

This is a vector drawing package that has been developed to draw, combine and manipulate objects and is an excellent tool for graphics modelling. The toolbar can be switched to a simple, configurable layout for younger pupils. '3-D Vector' clip art is supplied with *AspexDraw* to help pupils draw rooms in the home.

 Granada Draw (Granada Learning) – PC CD-ROM

This is a drawing program that allows pupils to create lines, shapes and other geometric drawings. These can range from simple plans to more complicated drawings of buildings and maps. As *Granada Draw* is vector-based, it gives pupils the opportunity to easily adjust, move and realign shapes they have created. Other features include shading, fills, rotation, scaling, a drawing grid and a legend. *Granada Draw* is fully configurable and can be used as a stand-alone application, or as an addition to the *Granada Toolkit*.

 SEMERC Draw (SEMERC) – PC CD-ROM

This is a new drawing program for Windows. This drawing package is fully configurable, allowing the teacher to add or remove tools as appropriate. The software will allow for elements of a drawing to be moved and scaled independently of the rest of the picture.

 VersaTile (Logotron) – PC CD-ROM

This allows pupils to determine the number of sides for polygons and explore tiling, symmetry, tessellation, pattern-making and design. *VersaTile* allows pupils to arrange these shapes without a grid and change the size and angle. The software includes examples from a range of cultures: for example African, Celtic, Greek, Indian, Islamic, Roman.

▼ Image-editing software

▶ KS 2 / P4–7

 Picture it! (Microsoft) – PC

Image-editing software which includes several videos as examples of projects. Pupils can change photograph colours, backgrounds or style, prepare montages of sets of photographs, add text, create decoupages and layered images. The software is easy to use, with good help facilities. It complements a paint package and allows pupils to import their own digital images or scanned images as well as being able to use prepared clip art.

▼ Computer-aided design

► KS 2 / P4–7

 Junior CAD (Soft Teach) – PC CD-ROM

This is designed to give pupils a taste of 3-D shape manipulation in design work. The shapes can be simple cubes through to a complex jet. Pupils can develop their own 3-D images or use the pre-drawn shapes for manipulation. The end product can be made using art straws and paper.

▼ Modelling

► KS 2 / P4–7

 Spex+ (Aspex Software) – Mac/Acorn/PC CD-ROM

This allows pupils to plan in 2-D then view in 3-D and comes with the materials to design a kitchen, a bathroom, a bedroom and a lounge. Pupils can use *Spex+* to design an environment, plan layout and arrange objects. They can also consider ergonomics, safety, style, colour, etc. Also included are photocopiable worksheets.

 tabs+ (Aspex Software) – PC CD-ROM

This is a 3-D design package for KS2/P4–7 through which pupils can design a model on-screen using basic shapes, view it in 3-D in wireframe or solid, turn and tumble the model, arrange nets of the model to best fit the paper, print or plot nets with tabs added ready to build a model of the design.

▼ Multimedia

► KS 1–2 / P4–7

 HyperStudio 4.0 (Knowledge Adventure inc) – Mac/PC CD-ROM

This is a multimedia authoring tool which allows pupils across the primary age range to create interactive presentations. It includes painting tools as well as text and graphics, with button actions that allow the inclusion of animation, video and sound. Pupils can use it at any stage of the primary age range to make presentations, create instruction programs, etc.

 Kid Pix Studio (Broderbund) – Mac/PC CD-ROM

This features all kinds of painting tools: dazzling multicolour fill patterns; scaleable construction brushes that build trees, brick walls, log cabins and more; hundreds of 'Animated Stamps' and 'Electric Mixer' effects. Three exciting new animation projects – Moopies, Stampimator and Digital Puppets – make it easy for pupils to add movement, video, sound effects and music to any picture or SlideShow production.

 StoryMaker (SPA Software) – PC CD-ROM

This is a very user-friendly and versatile multimedia authoring program which pupils can use effectively across the primary age range. It has banks of backgrounds and sprites suitable for primary topics. Sprites can be easily animated and sounds can be added to them. At a higher level, they can be made invisible and actions can be linked. Hyperlinks can be added to allow non-linear movement between pages. The computer will read any text inserted (or pasted) into speech bubbles. If colours are reduced to 256, the pupils' own

drawings can be pasted into *StoryMaker* pages and animated. Sound recorded by pupils in 'Sound Recorder' can be pasted into sprites. Primary site licenses are extremely competitively priced.

 TextEase Studio (Softease) – Mac/Acorn/PC CD-ROM

This includes a talking word processor, database, spreadsheet and desktop publishing programs. A very accessible software package, it also has a number of advanced features and it is very easy to drag and drop pictures, etc. The sound facility allows pupils to self-correct, as what they have written can be read back to them.

▶ KS 2 / P4–7

 Opus (previously called *Illuminatus*) (Digital Workshop) – PC CD-ROM

This is a sophisticated multimedia authoring program. It can be used effectively by upper KS2/P4-7 to produce impressive pages with, for example, automatic slide shows with special effects.

▼ Desktop publishing

▶ KS 1–2 / P1–7

 Clicker 4 (Cricksoft) – PC CD-ROM

This writing tool provides pupils with grids of words, pictures or words and pictures. Pupils can click in these grids to put a word or picture into the text. They can listen to the word first if they need to check that it is the correct one. Provides a 'way in' to desktop publishing.

 Granada Writer (Granada Learning) – PC CD-ROM

This is part of the *Granada Toolkit* and is a talking word processor featuring word, picture, sound and video banks. The desktop publishing facility will enable pupils to create their own web pages as well as design posters and banners.

 TextEase Studio (Softease) – Mac/Acorn/PC CD-ROM

Used as a desktop publishing program, *TextEase* allows pupils to insert graphic and photographic images into their document and insert text anywhere on the page. It is easy to use and has many of the more advanced tools, such as various text effects and drag and drop pictures. The talking version can read text back to pupils to help them spot errors.

▼ Music software

▶ KS 1–2 / P1–7

 Compose World Junior (ESP) – PC

This is a music exploration program where phrases of music are represented as pictures and/or words. These phrases can be any length and can contain both melody and harmony. The phrases are used as building blocks and can be sequenced in any order or combination. Compositions are produced by listening to your phrases and experimenting with different orders and combinations in the 'Sequencer'. *Compose World Junior* is a resource for exploring musical styles and developing listening and composition skills.

▼ CD-ROMs

▶ KS 1–2 / P1–7

 Encarta (Microsoft) – CD-ROM

This is a multimedia encyclopedia with excellent resources covering over 30,000 different topics. It has an interface with thousands of World Wide Web pages if used with a PC connected to the Internet.

▼ Internet

Internet access provides pupils with a wealth of materials from which they can research specific subjects they are studying. It also teaches them to be discriminating and to make judgements about the value of what they see and read. Schools can also set up their own website on which to display, among other things, Art projects they are involved in. Pupils can also use the e-mail facility to send copies of their work to other schools.

▼ Hardware resources

Digital cameras ▼

Digital cameras are an essential piece of equipment for the Art curriculum. They can be used:

- as a research tool;
- as a means of recording visual material and exploring new angles and viewpoints;
- as a means of investigating and exploring by creating montage, using part images and completing by hand;
- as a means of recording finished work for presentation via e-mail.

As a research tool, pupils can capture images of their immediate environment for further use in the classroom, for example on a visit to look at architectural styles in their area. The digital camera can also help them to focus in on detail to explore at a later date. Pupils also learn to 'look' at detail in more depth, changing angles, looking for interesting viewpoints and changing focus.

When images which have been photographed with the digital camera are imported into image-editing software, such as *Picture it!* (Microsoft), they can be altered, enhanced and overlaid to create interesting montages useful for inclusion in a sketchbook.

A computer with a fast processor and sufficient memory is ideal for processing and editing the images taken so that the process is not time-consuming and therefore frustrating for the pupils who are eager to see the results of their efforts.

Taking a good digital image is no different from taking a picture with an optical 35 mm camera, and the same rules for good picture-taking apply. The difference is that there is no film, the images being stored in the camera's memory. The software provided permits images to be viewed as thumbnails which resemble slides. Selecting all or some of the thumbnails and dragging the selection onto a directory on the hard disk downloads the full images and saves them. The exceptions to this are Sony Mavica cameras, whose images are stored in the form of JPEGs (compressed images) and saved directly onto floppy disks, which is very convenient for school use and compatible with Mac Power PCs as well as PC computers.

A collection of pupils' work photographed using a digital camera can quickly be sent via e-mail to a partner school for comment and appraisal, or posted onto a school website.

Scanners ▼

A scanner, in Art education, is useful as a means of inputting pupils' own work into the computer for further development using paint software. This applies to textile designs as well as paper-based projects. Any object which can comfortably fit onto the flatbed may be scanned and worked into, and the results printed for further development. As line drawings, photographs and text can be 'read' by a computer, in either black and white, greyscale or full colour, scanners are commonly used to import illustrations or photographs into a word processor or DTP program. The computer provides editing and manipulation facilities, eliminating the need to paste images physically into the text whilst maintaining the original in pristine condition. Material can also be inserted into on-line documents such as multimedia presentations.

The scan head and light source – located below the glass – automatically move down the document at a constant speed. Most low-cost flatbed scanners are designed to take A4 sheets, although A3 models are also available. Most measure approximately 400 x 300 x 100 mm, are quite sturdy, and have covers which hinge or adjust to allow you to scan bulky objects. 100 dpi (dots per inch) is usually quite sufficient resolution for most needs, as software can enlarge small images

considerably, although with some loss of quality.

To capture a scan, proceed as follows:

- Unless using a 'plug and play' device, switch on the scanner before switching on the computer so that the computer will recognise the device.
- Place the item to be copied face down on the scanner's glass bed and close the lid.
- Start the scanner software by clicking on the icon – it will generally say something like 'acquire and export' which will prompt you for a filename.
- The next step is to obtain a preview of the image, that is, a small version on which you can frame the part you want to scan.
- Once the preview image is on-screen a black frame appears with handles which allow you to move and resize it to section off all or some of the image for scanning.
- From the toolbar, select the required scanning resolution (usually 100–150 dpi) and the file format in which you want the resulting image (for example JPEG).
- Click on 'scan' and watch the image appear on-screen.
- If you are not happy at any time the scan can usually be interrupted, a new preview obtained and the frame readjusted.
- The final image can either be saved to a file or printed directly.

Art Links in the DfES/QCA ICT Scheme of Work ▼

Unit	ICT activity	Links with Art
1A	An introduction to modelling	Drawing ideas using vector-based graphics
1C	The information around us	CD research sources for project background and development
2B	Creating pictures	Developing design ideas graphically
2C	Finding information	CD-ROM, WWW research for projects
3A	Combining text and graphics	Poster design, leading to leaflet design and page layout
3B	Manipulating sound	Sound and picture journeys
3E	E-mail	Developing collaborative projects, research
4A	Writing for different audiences	Page layout design
4B	Developing images using repeating patterns	Textile design, printing fabric, etc.
5A	Graphical modelling	Drawing using object-based, graphics programs, textile designs, etc.
5B	Analysing data and asking questions: using complex searches	Research into the work of artists and designers
6A	Multimedia presentation	Study of movement, animation
6D	Using the Internet to search large databases and to interpret information	Research for projects, e.g. specific designers, styles, artists

As all aspects of ICT have become increasingly integrated into society and our schools, it becomes imperative to integrate the use and teaching of ICT across the curriculum.

The Scottish system, through its broad and varied curriculum, attempts to help all pupils find the area that is best suited to their talents. The use of ICT in Art and Design is a growing and exciting use of technology. It is being used for everything from Computer Aided Design (CAD) systems to the use of computer-generated graphics for film or presentation work.

Nelson Thornes' *Primary ICT Handbook Art and Design* reflects this need for ICT and not only introduces the skills needed but also develops them in an achievable and progressive way. It helps to fulfil many aspects of 5–14 Guidelines for ICT. In particular, it focuses coverage of the Creating and Presenting section.

Teachers are able to identify activities that support the strands using the ICT Handbooks website at www.nelsonthornes.com/primary/icthandbooks

There are six activities for each year group from Year R/P1 to Year 6/P7. In each year group, activities can be linked in pairs to the suggested projects given by the QCA for Art. For example, at the beginning of Year 3/P4, activities 19 and 20 refer to work carried out in project 3A of the Art Scheme of Work, activities 21 and 22 refer to the work you will be doing for project 3B, and so on. The activities are not designed exclusively for those projects, but will allow teachers to link ICT into Art more easily if they wish to. Activities also link to the work that pupils are doing in their ICT lessons in each year, if they are following a similar programme to that outlined in QCA Schemes of Work. Thus, in Year 4/P5, for example, they reuse and apply skills in activities 25–30 which they will have met in Unit 4B of the QCA scheme in their studies of pointillist art using dots of colour.

▼ Learning objectives

Each activity lists learning objectives which are related both to Art and ICT and will reflect those suggested by the QCA in the two subject Schemes of Work, and also those in the Scottish Guidelines for ICT. They allow pupils to reapply what they will have learned in an ICT lesson within the Art curriculum.

▼ ICT resources

Each activity lists resources in terms of computer software, but also suggests other artwork teachers may wish to have ready beforehand to use in the introduction to the activity. The software is not prescriptive. Activities are designed to be used with any paint package, since they all contain similar tools – colour palette, range of pencil tools, symmetry tool, etc.

▼ Organisation at the computer

As teachers choose an activity from those given, they should check the timing for that particular activity. Some are quite short and will allow for pairs of pupils to be rotated within one Art lesson, others will be more suitable for larger groups and take a longer period of time as the teacher works through an Art project with the rest of the class.

Activities Overview ▼

Learning objectives ▼

Pupils learn to:
- identify and create a circle or a square;
- use the 'paint can' tool to colour in primary colours;
- use the colour palette to choose a colour.

ICT resources ▼

Software such as *Granada Colours* (Granada Learning), *Dazzle Plus* (SEMERC) or similar paint package
Colour printer

Vocabulary ▼

shape
tool
cursor
click
drag

▼ Introduction

- Find round and square objects in class and group into the same colour, confining the choices to the three primary colours.
- Explain that pupils can make shapes on the computer and use the 'paint can' tool to fill in their shapes.
- Have ready a set of instructions and read through with the pupils. For example, '2 red squares and 2 blue circles'.

▼ Suggested activities

- Pupils open their paint package and choose the 'geometric shapes' menu.
- They create a circle, square or triangle, by clicking and dragging the mouse.
- Pupils repeat the activity until they have two squares and two circles (or two triangles).
- They click on the 'paint can' tool and then on a colour from the palette. They then click inside their shape to fill it with the colour.
- They then print their work, with help, and use it in the discussion.
- You may wish to change the number of shapes and use one, two or three colours according to the level of development of the pupils in the group.
- This is a starter activity which you can build on in following sessions.

▼ Assessment focus

Pupils can:
- use the 'geometric shapes' tools to create a circle, square or triangle;
- use the colour palette to choose a primary colour and use the 'paint can' tool to fill in their shape;
- read simple instructions.

2 Mix It Up ▼

Learning objectives ▼

Pupils learn to:
- identify and create a circle or a square;
- draw a shape part way over another shape;
- explore secondary colours by mixing two primaries.

ICT resources ▼

Software such as *Granada Colours* (Granada Learning), *Dazzle Plus* (SEMERC) or similar paint package with 'opacity' feature (Before you begin, find and set the opacity level to 80%. This allows pupils to see a mixture of two colours on computer.)
Colour printer

Vocabulary ▼

shape tool
click
drag
overlay

▼ Introduction

- Find groups of objects which are all the same colour: first red, then a set of yellow.
- Ask pupils if they can find an object which has these two colours mixed, i.e. an orange colour. Alternatively, demonstrate using paints what happens when the two colours are evenly mixed.
- Have ready a set of instructions for pupils and read through with them. For example, 'Make a red circle. Put a yellow circle over the top'. This will be their target.

▼ Suggested activities

- Pupils open their paint package and choose the 'geometric shapes' menu.
- They make a red circle or square, then repeat the activity, this time making a yellow shape and putting it over the red one, or part way over so that they can see the three colours.
- Pupils then print their work, with help, and use it in the discussion.
- Ask who made a red shape first, or a yellow one. Look at the printouts of those who started with red and added yellow, and then those who did it the other way round. Compare the two to see if there is any difference in the resulting mixed colour where the two overlap.

▼ Assessment focus

Pupils can:
- use the 'geometric shapes' tools to create a circle, square or triangle;
- use the colour palette to choose a primary colour and use the 'paint can' tool to fill in their shape;
- recognise secondary colours 'mixed' on computer.

Learning objectives ▼

Pupils learn to:
- use the 'pencil' tool to create thick and thin lines;
- create a pattern of lines of different types;
- explore the use of different colours of lines.

ICT resources ▼

Software such as *Granada Colours* (Granada Learning) or similar paint package
Colour printer

Vocabulary ▼

pencil tool
freehand

▼ Introduction

- Draw different types of lines on the board: thick, thin, wavy, zigzag, broken, etc.
- Ask volunteers to draw one of the lines you have made.
- Explain that pupils can experiment with different types of line on the computer.
- Prepare cards for pupils if you feel that they need support, but allow them to experiment with their own combinations as well.

▼ Suggested activities

- Pupils open their paint package and choose the 'freehand pencil' tool.
- They right click on the tool to learn that the higher the number, the thicker the line they can draw.
- They then create their lines across the screen in their chosen pattern, or follow your prepared card.
- Pupils can make a series of straight lines in different thicknesses, create a pattern of thick and thin wavy lines, or a mixture of all types you have discussed.
- Pupils can change colour at any time by using the colour palette.
- Some pupils may need to have a prepared screen to guide them for the zigzag lines, as this needs fine mouse control.
- Pupils then print their work, with help, and use it in the discussion.
- This is an activity you can use and develop throughout the year for mouse control and use of colour, and which also helps with the Fireworks activity (p.27).

▼ Assessment focus

Pupils can:
- control the mouse to create a series of lines;
- create a pattern of lines of different shapes and thicknesses;
- use more than one colour in a pattern.

4 Fireworks ▼

Learning objectives ▼

Pupils learn to:
- change the background colour of the screen;
- create a picture using the 'freehand pencil' tool;
- explore the use of different colours of lines against a dark background.

ICT resources ▼

Software such as *Granada Colours* (Granada Learning) or similar paint package
Colour printer

Vocabulary ▼

background
screen
freehand pencil tool

▼ Introduction

- Show some printed copies of pupils' other work on lines and ask if they remember the types of lines they used.
- Show photographs of firework displays, postcards or posters and talk about the colours used, and also the background.
- Prepare cards for pupils if you feel that they need support, giving them the order of working on-screen, to create the background first and then choose their bright colours for the fireworks.

▼ Suggested activities

- Pupils open their paint package and click to choose the 'paint can' tool.
- They then click on a colour and anywhere on screen to change the background.
- Pupils choose the 'freehand pencil' tool and a colour from the palette to start to create their lines of fireworks.
- Some pupils may find it easier to use the 'pencil' tool which automatically draws a straight line, as this is easier to control.
- Pupils can also make a Catherine wheel by making circular movements with the mouse.
- Pupils can change colour at any time by clicking on another colour from the palette.
- They then print their work, with help, and use it in the discussion.
- Ask about background colours – black or dark blues, and talk about pupils' choices and the types of lines they have used, comparing different printouts.

▼ Assessment focus

Pupils are able to:
- change the colour of the background;
- create a picture using a series of freehand lines;
- talk about the type of line they have used and the mixture of colours.

5 Repeating the Shapes ▼

Learning objectives ▼

Pupils learn to:
- arrange shapes to form a pattern;
- click and drag using the mouse;
- identify two shapes in a pattern repeat.

ICT resources ▼

Software such as *Granada Writer,*
MyWorld 4 (both Granada
Learning) or *Talking First Word*
(Research Machines)
Colour printer

Vocabulary ▼

pattern
repeat
click
drag
shape

▼ Introduction

- Remind pupils of a circle, square and triangle, and then place shapes on a desk in a repeat of one primary colour and two shapes, for example red square, red circle, red square, red circle.
- Explain to pupils that they will first arrange five shapes of one colour into a pattern on the computer screen.
- Prepare two screens – one with a set of five shapes, and one with a set of six of each of the three basic shapes.
- Then they will work on two shapes and make a repeat like the ones you have demonstrated.
- Prepare instruction cards for pupils if you feel that they need support, but allow them to experiment with their own combinations as well.

▼ Suggested activities

- Pupils open a prepared screen with five squares, circles or triangles given.
- They choose a shape and drag it to their chosen position.
- Pupils repeat the activity until they have arranged the shapes in a pattern on-screen.
- They then open a prepared screen with six of each shape – square, triangle and circle – all in the same colour.
- They can now click and drag to create their own repeated patterns.
- Pupils then print their work, with help, and use it in the discussion.
- Check that they can all click and drag competently, and count the number of shapes they have used to check that they have understood how to create a repeat.

▼ Assessment focus

Pupils can:
- click and drag objects around the screen;
- create a pattern of one shape and one colour;
- create a repeat pattern in one colour but with different shapes.

6 Turn the Shapes Around ▼

Learning objectives ▼

Pupils learn to:
- rotate a shape on-screen;
- create a pattern repeat with a rotation of a triangle;
- use more than one colour in a pattern repeat.

ICT resources ▼

Software such as *Granada Writer,*
MyWorld 4 (both Granada
Learning) or *Talking First Word*
(Research Machines)
Colour printer

Vocabulary ▼

pattern
rotation
repeat

▼ Introduction

- Show pupils a circle and a triangle, then turn the circle and ask if the shape 'changes' its appearance.
- Do the same with the triangle and ask the same question.
- Place the two shapes on a desk in a repeat of one primary colour, but turn the triangle upside down for every other repeat of that shape.
- Explain that pupils will first arrange their pattern on-screen, then learn how to rotate every other triangle.
- Prepare a screen with 10 circles and 10 triangles, in one or more colours.
- Prepare instruction cards for pupils who need support, but allow them to experiment with their own combinations as well.

▼ Suggested activities

- Pupils open the prepared screen.
- They choose a shape, then drag it to their chosen position to arrange the shapes in a repeat pattern.
- They then double click on each triangle they wish to turn, and use the mouse to rotate it.
- You can prepare screens with a variety of shapes according to pupils' ability – use more than one colour, and confine to one shape or mix both colours and shapes for more able pupils.
- Pupils then print their work, with help, and use it in the discussion.
- Ask pupils in class how they turned their shape, and count the number they have used to check that they have understood how to create a repeat.

▼ Assessment focus

Pupils can:
- choose and turn an object on-screen;
- create a pattern repeat which has a rotated image;
- use more than one colour in a pattern repeat.

Learning objectives ▼

Pupils learn to:
- make marks using the 'pencil' tool;
- explore mark-making with other tools to represent pastel or charcoal;
- create different textures to represent clothing or hair for portraits.

ICT resources ▼

Software such as *Granada Colours* (Granada Learning), *Dazzle Plus* (SEMERC) or similar paint package
Colour printer
Learning resources: pupils' photographs

Vocabulary ▼

tool
brush
pencil tool
pencil size
colour palette

▼ Introduction

- Discuss the different ways in which pupils are represented in images you have collected.
- Encourage pupils to talk about the images, leading towards comments on what the image tells us about the subject's character.
- Explore in more depth how the artist or photographer has achieved the effects by use of line and colour in particular.

▼ Suggested activities

- Pupils open their paint package and select the 'pencil' tool.
- They make straight, curved and broken lines across the screen, using click and drag.
- Pupils then alter the thickness of their line and change from round to square or vice versa.
- Pupils then start to explore how this technique could be used for hair or clothing – you could also include cross-hatching as a technique here.
- Pupils may also change the colour of the line by selecting from the palette.
- Pupils save and print a copy of their experiments, and compare their mark-making with that done by hand.
- Ask pupils to describe how they might make use of their experiments for a portrait. Encourage them to link style of lines to character.

▼ Assessment focus

Pupils:
- understand how to use the 'pencil' tool in differing thicknesses and styles;
- have a range of vocabulary to describe their mark-making;
- can relate choice of line to style of portrait.

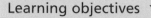

8 Objects and Colour in Portraits ▼

Learning objectives ▼

Pupils learn to:
* make darker or lighter tones of colour, using the 'colour cycle' and 'spray gun';
* make more links between style of portrait and character;
* arrange objects on the page to make a clear record of observations and experiments.

ICT resources ▼

Software such as *Granada Colours* (Granada Learning), *Dazzle Plus* (SEMERC) or similar paint package with 'colour cycle' facility
Colour printer

Vocabulary ▼

tone
tint
grades
spray gun
colour cycle

▼ Introduction

* Explore and discuss how artists use objects to portray status, events and interests of their subjects in portraits you have collected.
* Encourage pupils to talk about what they would include in a portrait of themselves. Ask them to collect images they would like to use.
* Relate also the overall effect of a portrait to the use of ranges of colours which are warm or cold, and reflect a range of feelings – anger, fear, joy.
* Explain that pupils will explore ranges of colours on computer and then add clip art they have chosen, as part of a sketchbook project to prepare for their own portrait.

▼ Suggested activities

* Pupils open their paint package and select the 'colour cycle'.
* They choose a colour range and then 'paint' across the screen at different speeds to look at how the range of colours changes.
* Pupils explore how they may 'break up' these lines of colour using the 'spray gun' to create 'dots' of colour over their original.
* They then select clip art from the image bank and add objects over their colour experiments.
* Pupils save and print a copy of their experiments, as preparation for future portrait work.
* Ask pupils to explain why they chose what they did and how the objects and colours form a background for character within the portrait.

▼ Assessment focus

Pupils:
* understand how to use the 'colour cycle' and 'spray gun' to create mood and feelings;
* can add clip art to portray important objects;
* can relate their experiments to their portrait work.

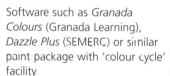

Learning objectives ▼

Pupils learn to:
- make a coloured background which will form a weft;
- experiment with paper weaving techniques;
- learn more about how warp and weft relate to each other in terms of colour and design.

ICT resources ▼

Software such as *Granada Colours* (Granada Learning), *Dazzle Plus* (SEMERC) or similar paint package
Colour printer

Vocabulary ▼

horizontal
vertical
straight line tool
paint can

▼ Introduction

- Discuss the composition of woven fabrics which you have collected, looking carefully at warp and weft.
- Discuss differences in fabrics seen close up and at a distance. Do the colours blend?
- Use a card loom to demonstrate the basic technique and to show pupils that the warp colour may have different effects on the overall design, depending on how much the warp shows in the final pattern.
- Explain that pupils will explore on computer ways in which to prepare a coloured background which they can cut and weave as a weft thread.

▼ Suggested activities

- Pupils open their paint package and select the 'straight line' tool.
- They make a series of lines across the screen to divide it into sections – horizontal or diagonal stripes – then use the 'paint can' to add colour, staying with one range.
- Pupils print and cut their paper into strips, then weave them first into white, to see how the colour is broken up into squares, then into a chosen colour which matches or contrasts with their paper weft.
- Some pupils may want to experiment by going 'over 2 under 1'. They can then compare the effect of a finished piece in terms of colour 'saturation'.
- Ask pupils to explain how their weaving has changed.
- Use this time to reinforce the concept that the result of their weaving gives them blocks of colour that can be broken down into squares.

▼ Assessment focus

Pupils:
- understand how to use the computer to experiment with designs for weaving;
- can weave paper in a variety of ways;
- can talk about the different effects of their woven pieces.

 YEAR 1 / P2

10 Designing with Squares ▼

Learning objectives ▼

Pupils learn to:
- use the computer to plan a design;
- experiment with different weaving techniques on the computer screen;
- prepare a series of designs, comparing each different technique.

ICT resources ▼

Software such as *Granada Colours* (Granada Learning), *Dazzle Plus* (SEMERC) or similar paint package
Colour printer
Learning resources: Fair Isle knitting pattern or similar to show design in squares

Vocabulary ▼

brush size

▼ Introduction

- Ask pupils to compare the results of weaving with threads and with paper.
- Use their paper weaving to return to the idea that the piece can be seen as a construction of squares of colour in different proportions.
- Explain that pupils can prepare designs in this way on the computer. Show them a Fair Isle knitting pattern, where the design is given in squares.

▼ Suggested activities

- Pupils open their paint package and choose a square brush in a large size.
- They draw the vertical lines for their warp in their chosen colour.
- They then choose another colour to start their weft and click once each time to create a square over their weft in an 'over 1 under 1' pattern, for four rows of weaving.
- Pupils then create a series of 'over 2 under 2' lines underneath.
- They repeat with the same warp colour, but change the weft.
- They save and print their work for discussion.
- Ask pupils to explain how the effect of their weaving has changed, depending on their use of different numbers of 'over' threads.
- Ask them also what difference it makes if you use the same warp colour but change the weft.
- Can pupils understand how the computer may be used as a way of planning some weaving?

▼ Assessment focus

Pupils:
- understand how to use the computer to experiment with designs for weaving;
- can create a plan for a possible weaving project;
- understand the differences between 'over 1 under 1' and 'over 2 under 2' in the final design.

Learning objectives ▼

Pupils will:
- understand more about the range of materials used for sculpture;
- understand the difference between durable and temporary;
- choose a page from an open Internet site with guidance.

ICT resources ▼

Internet
Printer
Learning resources: objects in materials you wish pupils to explore: cartons, paper, fabric

Vocabulary ▼

Internet
log on
search

▼ Introduction

- Explain that the computer is a store of information, and that the Internet is like having access to a large library.
- Tell pupils that each address is like a section in the library, and that you are going to find a section on sculpture.
- Log on to the Internet with one group of pupils at a time, showing them how the computer telephones its large library and asks to be allowed into the section.
- Type in the design museum address: www.designmuseum.org.

▼ Suggested activities

- Look down the subjects listed. There are articles on sculptors and materials.
- Read through some of the entries on materials and ask pupils if they have seen these materials in school or at home.
- Pupils click on an entry for materials and scroll down to see the variety of objects made from that material.
- Pupils then compare objects in metal or wood with the cartons or paper you have collected.
- Let pupils touch each and describe what would happen if, for example, the carton and the metal were put in water. This will help pupils to understand more about the longer durability of some materials.
- Discuss other uses of the computer for research. What sort of things might pupils find out from this site?
- How would it help them with a future sculpture?

▼ Assessment focus

Pupils:
- understand that the Internet is like a large library and contains useful ideas for research;
- understand more about durability;
- can choose a page from an index within an open site with guidance.

12 Sculpture ▼

Learning objectives ▼

Pupils learn how to:
- collect images and colours as starting points for sculpture;
- relate the materials and colours they choose to their feelings about an environment;
- explore the use of collage on computer to help to develop ideas.

ICT resources ▼

Software such as *Dazzle Plus* (SEMERC), *Granada Colours* (Granada Learning) or similar paint package
Corel Clip Art Gallery or similar collection of clip art
Colour printer

Vocabulary ▼

collage
spray can
geometric shapes tools
freehand pencil tool
paint can

▼ Introduction

- Talk to pupils about a recent visit they have made to a park, garden, river or nature trail.
- Concentrate on the colours and textures that they saw and felt. Help pupils to describe how they felt.
- Explain that pupils will use the computer to collect different pictures which will create a mood board, not a representation, of a forest, seaside scene or river scene.
- Show an example of a 'mood' board: a selection of colours, shapes and textures which all give an impression of comfort, warmth, happiness, freedom. Show a mixture of pictures of flowers, trees, blocks of colour and parts of surfaces with moss, grass or rocks, all to be found in a good clip art collection.

▼ Suggested activities

- Pupils open their paint package and begin to import pictures or textural clip art from their clip art package.
- They also create blocks of colour, using either the 'geometric shapes' tools or the 'freehand pencil' tool, and then the paint can to block fill.
- Encourage pupils to experiment with a collage which just gives them the feeling of being in the place they visited, rather than actually looking like it.
- Some pupils will be able to work over the clip art with the spray can for example, to create further layers of texture.
- Pupils save and print a copy of their work.
- Discuss pupils' use of images, colour and texture. Ask why pupils placed images where they did, and also comment on relative sizes of images.

▼ Assessment focus

Pupils can:
- understand more about the use of colour and shape to create mood;
- use a range of tools in a paint package and import clip art;
- talk about their work and make positive criticism of the compositions of others.

13 What's the Angle? ▼

Learning objectives ▼

Pupils learn to:
- make a collage of photographs;
- overlay their images;
- crop images;
- create interesting compositions.

ICT resources ▼

Software such as *Granada Writer* (Granada Learning), *TextEase* (Softease) or *Microsoft Word* (Microsoft)
Clip art photo files
Scanner
Learning resources: photographs from family albums; newspapers and magazines

Vocabulary ▼

angle
composition
layout
collage
crop

▼ Introduction

- Look at a selection of family photographs.
- Decide with pupils which *parts* of the photos are most interesting – for example it may be just a head of a figure, or an expression or a setting which is important.
- Discuss where the photographer was standing/sitting/lying when the photographs were taken – use *angle* in your discussions.
- Show pupils a prepared, handmade collage of your own family.
- Explain that pupils can prepare this form of collage on computer, and will work on a theme of 'Friendship'.

▼ Suggested activities

- Pupils choose sets of images which they feel represent themselves as a friendship group.
- Help them to scan images, or encourage them to use clip art.
- Pupils import a collection of images into a DTP package such as *Granada Writer*.
- They overlay their images using 'bring to front' or 'send to back' as controls.
- If using software such as *Word*, pupils may use the 'crop' tool to select parts of their image and then overlay in the same way.
- If pupils are more advanced they may add text to their collage, or letters flood-filled in colours.
- Pupils present their collage, either on-screen or as a printed copy, and generate a discussion about the chosen images and the layout.

▼ Assessment focus

Pupils can:
- select and overlay images to make interesting compositions;
- crop images, leaving relevant and interesting parts;
- talk about the mood of their composition.

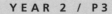

14 Moody Blues ▼

Learning objectives ▼

Pupils learn to:
- explore the use of different letter forms;
- use the 'flood fill' tool;
- make a collage of colour and shape to express their feelings.

ICT resources ▼

Software such as *Granada Draw* (Granada Learning), *Dazzle Plus* (SEMERC) or similar art package; *Granada Writer* (Granada Learning) or similar DTP package
Learning resources: magazine illustrations with a strong element of colour for mood; copy of 'Violin' by Picasso

Vocabulary ▼

flood fill
font
collage

▼ Introduction

- Discuss the use of colour in some magazine illustrations. Use images which have a measure of symbolism rather than representation – individual words, colour, images as a collage. Picasso's 'Violin' composition is a good example of this type of work.
- Refer pupils to the colour wheel and discuss the moods various sides of the wheel can represent.
- Ask pupils to look at combinations of colours from the same side of the wheel – red, orange, yellow, for example.
- Discuss the use of different styles of letters and their purpose.

▼ Suggested activities

- Pupils work on one of a given set of themes – loneliness, celebration, nightmare or peace, for example.
- They open the art package and choose images from the clip art collection which 'suggest' their theme.
- Pupils experiment with letter forms, finding fonts which they can enlarge and flood fill.
- As pupils arrive at words or images which they want to keep, they select the area and copy it so that they can put it into *Granada Writer* or a similar DTP package to make their collage.
- Ask pupils to show their work on-screen or as a printed copy and discuss what images they have chosen and why.
- Encourage pupils to accept feedback and ideas from the class so that they can return to and develop their work at a later stage.

▼ Assessment focus

Pupils can:
- understand how to work with different font styles;
- use the 'flood fill' tool;
- create a collage;
- talk about their use of colour, shape and pattern to represent an event.

Learning objectives ▼

Pupils learn to:
- use the geometric tools to create shape;
- create a stamp for repeated images;
- use special effects to change texture.

ICT resources ▼

Software such as *Granada Colours* (Granada Learning), *Dazzle Plus* (SEMERC) or similar paint package
Colour printer
Clip art photographs of buildings
Scanner
Learning resources: pupils' own drawings of parts of buildings

Vocabulary ▼

effects
select an area
geometric
stamp

▼ Introduction

- Pupils study a small part of a drawing or photograph of part of a building, wall, roof, pattern or grain of wood.
- Encourage pupils to look for a repeated shape, for example the trapeze of tiles on a roof, or rectangles in a brick wall.
- Look at regular repeats and patterns (bricks) and compare with more irregular ones (stone wall). Here are some examples.

▼ Suggested activities

- Pupils open their paint package.
- They insert clip art of a building, or use a scanned image of their own drawing.
- Pupils use the 'pen' tool to draw the shape they find within the drawing, or the 'geometric shapes' tools to create a pattern.
- They use the 'create a stamp' function so that they can repeat the image they have drawn.
- Pupils then select their repeated pattern and use the 'effects' part of the package to create a mosaic, a ripple effect or an embossed effect.
- Ask questions. Which shapes were best to use and why? Which pattern was most successful? What could you do next with your printed work?

▼ Assessment focus

Pupils:
- understand how to create a stamp;
- can use the 'geometric shapes' tools;
- understand how to create an abstract pattern from their own drawing or found image.

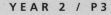 **YEAR 2 / P3**

16 Underneath the Arches ▼

Learning objectives ▼

Pupils learn to:
- insert clip art;
- make a collage;
- crop images to select specific parts.

ICT resources ▼

Software such as *Granada Colours* (Granada Learning), *Dazzle Plus* (SEMERC) or similar paint package
Colour printer
Learning resources: photographs of different styles of buildings

Vocabulary ▼

select
deselect
lasso tool

▼ Introduction

- Look at photographs of buildings, concentrating on a selection of different features such as doorways or windows.
- Encourage pupils to use a viewfinder to select different parts of the images, concentrating on interesting shapes or textures.
- Explain that pupils can use the computer to do the same thing.

▼ Suggested activities

- Pupils open their paint package.
- They insert clip art of a building and select a part of the picture, as they did with the viewfinder.
- Pupils then save this selected image to a new document, which they will file as 'their name + collage' and then repeat the exercise, saving each new selection to their collage file. They can move the new image around as much as they wish before they 'deselect' it. Once in place it has to be reselected using the 'lasso' tool before it can be moved again.
- Pupils then arrange their chosen selections in different ways to form a collage of one particular element. They reselect one image from their collage file and move it to change the balance of the screen or overlap another image if they wish.
- Pupils describe why they have chosen their particular elements.
- Do all the parts of the collage reflect the same aspect – texture, shape, pattern?
- Have pupils chosen a range of different things? Why?

▼ Assessment focus

Pupils:
- understand how to insert clip art;
- know how to select different areas of their screen;
- understand how to build a collage;
- can discuss different choices using the correct vocabulary.

Learning objectives ▼

Pupils learn to:
• insert clip art;
• use the 'select an area' tool;
• use the 'flip X' and 'flip Y' controls;
• tile their work to make an overall pattern.

ICT resources ▼

Software such as *Granada Colours* (Granada Learning), *Dazzle Plus* (SEMERC) or similar paint package (Find the clip art sections for natural forms and let pupils have the folder titles.)
Colour printer
Learning resources: examples of wallpaper, carpet, curtain designs using natural forms, e.g. William Morris, Laura Ashley

Vocabulary ▼

rotate
select an area
flip X
flip Y
pattern
tile

▼ Introduction

• Discuss the use of different sorts of patterns in the work of William Morris or Laura Ashley.
• Show patterns of natural forms which have been turned upside down or rotated horizontally.
• Use a viewfinder to select one flower or a pair which have been rotated in some way.

▼ Suggested activities

• Pupils open their paint package, create a new document and click on the 'clip art' file.
• They open a file on natural forms, under a title such as flowers, plants or trees.
• Pupils choose a flower and import it into their personal document.
• They insert two images of their flower.
• Pupils select one flower using the 'select an area' tool. Once the image is selected, pupils use the appropriate tool to turn the image either horizontally or vertically.
• Pupils then click on 'select an area' again to grab both pictures.
• They then go to 'area' and 'tile'. They will see their image repeated across the whole screen.
• Pupils can select another area from their overall pattern and tile again. What happens? Does the space around each flower make a difference?

▼ Assessment focus

Pupils:
• understand how to repeat a pattern;
• know how to select different areas of their screen;
• understand rotations vertically;
• can discuss the different patterns using correct vocabulary;
• can say where they might apply this skill in design.

Learning objectives ▼

Pupils learn to:
- draw using the 'freehand pencil' tool;
- use the 'flood fill' tool;
- use the 'geometric shapes' tools;
- select and tile their work to make an overall pattern.

ICT resources ▼

Software such as *Granada Colours* (Granada Learning), *Dazzle Plus* (SEMERC) or similar paint package
Colour printer
Learning resources: examples of wallpaper, carpet, curtain designs using natural forms, but shown in abstract

Vocabulary ▼

flip X
flip Y
pattern
tile

▼ Introduction

- Look at modern geometric designs for wallpapers and curtains, e.g. from Ikea or Habitat.
- Ask pupils to identify circle, triangle or square. Ask if the flowers they have already used suggest a shape (daisy is triangular, buttercup circular).
- Explain that pupils will use the same techniques as in the previous activity to tile shapes, but that this time they will first make their own 'flowers'.

▼ Suggested activities

- Pupils open their paint package, and click on the 'geometric shapes' tools.
- They draw a chosen shape on-screen. Click to start, drag to size and click to stop.
- They may use the 'freehand pencil' tool for the stem, and the 'diamond' tool for leaves.
- Pupils then go to the 'paint can' in the 'tools' menu, select it and select a colour.
- They click within their shapes to flood fill.
- Clicking on another colour in the colour palette will change the colour.
- Pupils then click on 'select an area' again to select their coloured flower.
- They then go to 'area' and 'tile and half drop' this time, or 'tile and flip'.
- Ask what happens if they shorten the stems and flip horizontally or if they mix 'real' flowers with the shapes.

▼ Assessment focus

Pupils:
- understand how to use the 'geometric shapes' tools and 'freehand pencil' tool;
- know how to select different areas of their screen;
- understand how to use the 'flood fill' tool.

Learning objectives ▼

Pupils learn to:
• adapt line and colour from an artist's work to form a background;
• scan an image with support and select a part of it using the 'lasso' tool;
• superimpose figures onto their background using scanned images.

ICT resources ▼

Software such as *Granada Colours* (Granada Learning) or similar paint package
Scanner
Colour printer

Vocabulary ▼

scan
select
lasso
superimpose

▼ Introduction

• Ask pupils to study paintings or photographs of couples and to describe the mood or relationship between the people, concentrating on the use of line and colour to help in portraying this mood.
• Van Gogh's skies or Munch's 'Scream' show graphically how the use of line helps the mood of the portraits or landscapes.
• Explain that pupils can create this sort of background on computer using the 'freehand pencil' tool for the line, and the 'flood fill' for the colour.
• Ask pupils to think about families of colours for a harmonious effect, or contrasting colours which may produce a more jarring, angry effect.

▼ Suggested activities

• Pupils work on their background as outlined above and save it into their personal or class folder.
• They then copy and paste a scanned image into their art package, using the 'lasso' tool to choose a part of the image, a face or figure.
• Once in place, the image cannot be moved without moving the background as well. If pupils want to change its position they can do so by clicking on 'undo' and then repeating the process.
• Discuss the finished screens or printed copies. Pupils tell others what they have chosen and why. How does this depict the mood or the relationship between the two figures in their composition?

▼ Assessment focus

Pupils can:
• scan an image with help;
• prepare a background, concentrating on colour and line;
• import part of an image onto a prepared background;
• talk about the mood of their composition.

20 Portraits for Character ▼

Learning objectives ▼

Pupils learn to:
- interpret abstract portraits, describing character from use of colour and line;
- use the 'line' and 'flood fill' tools to create their own abstract portraits;
- discuss their own work in relation to that of other artists.

ICT resources ▼

Software such as *Granada Colours* (Granada Learning) or similar paint package
Scanner
Colour printer

Vocabulary ▼

flood fill
freehand pencil
straight line pencil

▼ Introduction

- Study paintings by Picasso (e.g. 'Woman Weeping') and ask pupils how they think the artist has created the mood or character.
- Draw out from their discussions the use of line and colour to help in portraying this mood.
- Explain that pupils can create this style of portrait on computer.
- Demonstrate to groups if you feel it is necessary.
- Ask pupils to think of how they might portray an angry or happy person in this style. Suggest that they create a portrait to show either an argument or a celebration.

▼ Suggested activities

- Pupils use the 'straight line pencil' and 'flood fill' tools to help them with this project, also adding geometric shapes if they feel it will be useful.
- You could scan part of the portrait by Picasso and ask pupils to complete a part of it by looking at the original.
- Pupils then work on placing figures into a background, in the same style.
- They could use scanned images or clip art in a more representational style, and mix the two, for example a playground scene or wedding scene for the celebration.
- Encourage pupils to be as inventive as possible, and to move away from the idea that the picture needs to represent people or places realistically.
- Take time to discuss the finished screens. Pupils can discuss their use of colour, background and the reasons they mixed abstract and representational.

▼ Assessment focus

Pupils can:
- create an abstract portrait which conveys feelings;
- use the 'flood fill' and 'pencil' tools in more depth;
- Create a background which shows the situation in which the figures are placed;
- relate their work to that of the artist under study.

21 Symmetry and Pattern

Learning objectives ▼

Pupils learn to:
- use the 'symmetry' tool in a paint package;
- create a symmetrical pattern in geometric style;
- relate their work to Islamic art and to surface pattern designs available for decoration.

ICT resources ▼

Software such as *Granada Colours* (Granada Learning) or similar paint package
Scanner
Colour printer

Vocabulary ▼

flood fill
symmetry
geometric
zoom

▼ Introduction

- Show pupils carpet designs from the Middle East, and/or wallpaper, fabric or carpet designs which are geometric.
- Place a mirror along the line of symmetry of a design and ask pupils to look at the reflection and at the other side of the mirror to see that they are the same.
- Discuss different lines of symmetry – vertical and horizontal two-way and a four-way symmetrical pattern.

▼ Suggested activities

- Pupils begin with half a ready-prepared simple pattern and complete the other half.
- They then use the 'symmetry' tool in their paint package which helps them to create the pattern simultaneously. If you are studying Islamic art, remind pupils that there will be no pictures in their design, only geometric shapes.
- Pupils start with a two-way design, then work on a more complex four-way symmetry.
- When pupils have completed their first pattern, encourage them to use the 'flood fill' tool to add colour. This will not be added to both parts of the pattern at once.
- Encourage pupils to think of the negative spaces between their shapes.
- If pupils find that they fill the screen very quickly, and that the shapes are large, they can use the 'zoom' tool to make the screen larger to work in more detail.
- As pupils complete their patterns, encourage them to begin to think about where this might be used (for textiles/wall hangings).

▼ Assessment focus

Pupils can:
- use the 'symmetry' tool to create pattern in a given style;
- use the 'flood fill' tool to add colour to both positive and negative shapes;
- talk about their patterns and their possible uses, and relate their work to that of other craftspeople.

Learning objectives ▼

Pupils learn to:
- use the 'tile and drop' and 'half drop' functions of a paint package;
- create a pattern suitable for further repeats to create a length of fabric;
- rotate images to create more complex pattern repeats;
- relate their work to surface pattern designs available for decoration.

ICT resources ▼

Software such as *Granada Colours* (Granada Learning) or similar paint package
Scanner
Colour printer

Vocabulary ▼

tile
drop
half drop
rotations
flip

▼ Introduction

- Have ready examples of designs for fabric with clear but complex repeats, e.g. William Morris. Find a complex geometric pattern repeat as a contrast.
- Discuss in more detail the use of repeats, pointing out to pupils that there are rotations of patterns within the repeat and that the line of repeat is not always completely vertical, but can be slightly offset to form a wavy line of images.
- Draw the line of the repeat on the board so that pupils can see how the pattern was constructed.
- Explain that pupils will use the computer to try out patterns containing three images, one in rotation.
- They can take natural forms as their subject or choose a theme such as sport for a wallpaper.

▼ Suggested activities

- Pupils choose their theme from the clip art available. Direct them to a choice of three or four areas.
- They import three images as clip art, then use the 'select an area' tool to select and rotate one or more of them.
- Once pupils have the images together, one rotated, they 'select' them with the 'rectangle select' tool and try 'tile and half drop' and 'tile and flip', to give them an overall screen pattern.
- Pupils then work into their pattern using the 'flood fill' tool, or the 'spray can'.
- They can then print two copies of the print to test whether or not it will make a successful repeat.

▼ Assessment focus

Pupils can:
- use the 'select an area' tool to rotate an image;
- use the 'tile and flip' and 'tile and half drop' tools to create full-screen patterns.

Learning objectives ▼

Pupils learn to:
- apply their knowledge of composition to a new area of design;
- import photographs of gardens to a drawing package;
- create a composite image with appropriate sound as part of a garden design.

ICT resources ▼

Software such as *Granada Colours* (Granada Learning) or similar paint package; *Granada Writer* (Granada Learning) or similar DTP package; *Compose World Junior* (ESP) or similar composition package
Learning resources: video

Vocabulary ▼

composition
composite image
sound file

▼ Introduction

- Show video extracts of visits to different styles of gardens or sculpture parks.
- Discuss the sounds, either natural or man-made, to be found in these parks and gardens.
- Explain to pupils that designers often create water features incorporating the sound of the water as part of the design. Other designers use sculpture in metal to make sounds in the wind, or use oriental wind-chimes.
- Ask pupils to discuss the effects of such features on the visitor to a garden.
- Show pupils a selection of photographs of gardens or parks which you have collected and scanned into the computer.
- Decide in groups what sort of effect pupils might like to create using a range of sounds available in their musical composition package.

▼ Suggested activities

- Pupils open their paint package and import one or more of the scanned photographs. Offer them the choice of importing other objects or flowers which they might like to place in their garden.
- They save their work to personal folders and open *Compose World Junior*. There are several sets of natural sounds of wind and water in this package for pupils to use.
- Pupils compose a series of sounds suitable for their garden collage, thinking about shapes and colours as well as natural sounds of water.
- They then import the collage and sounds into a DTP document.
- Did any groups try to relate the colour and sound, and if so with what result? Did some groups focus on the shape of their garden or on one object to begin their composition and again, what were the results?

▼ Assessment focus

Pupils can:
- use a composition package;
- create a collage for a garden or park;
- relate their choice of sounds to shape, colour or mood of their garden or park setting.

24 Grouping Objects in a Planned Landscape ▼

Learning objectives ▼

Pupils learn to:
- create an aerial view of a landscape plan;
- use their plan to create a small model;
- alter and amend their designs based on discussion of their 3-D plan.

ICT resources ▼

Software such as *Granada Draw* (Granada Learning) or similar vector drawing package

Vocabulary ▼

symmetry
offset

▼ Introduction

- Have ready examples of oriental-style garden designs.
- Discuss in more detail the use of symmetry, the use of one vivid object in an otherwise plain setting, the use of water, stone, and the importance of positioning so that the elements can be viewed successfully from different viewpoints.
- Explain to pupils the use of shrubs and trees in groups of three in a triangular format, and how this avoids straight lines. This can also extend to other objects such as a bridge, tree and large rock.
- Encourage pupils to offer alternatives to some of the designs you show them, asking them always to explain why they would move an element.
- Explain that pupils will begin to plan their own garden design in this style on computer as an aerial view, test it with 3-D models, and then amend the design.
- Suggest the number of elements to help some pupils to make a clearer start, for example, a stream, a waterfall, a tree, a bridge, a large rock and three plants of one or more colours.

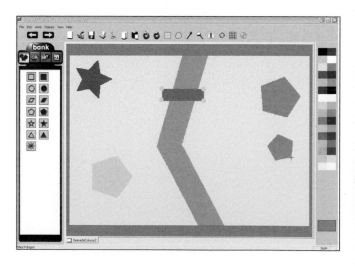

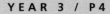

▼ Suggested activities

- Pupils open their drawing package, and use the 'geometric shapes' tools to create each element of their garden, with a key if you have specified this.
- They plan their layout, taking into account different viewpoints. Pupils can use a straight line from different angles to check on what will be seen, and amend their plans accordingly.
- Pupils save and print copies of their work and then try out ideas with small models.
- They will need to check at eye level whether their first ideas on computer prove workable and provide a harmonious design, equally pleasing from different angles as visitors walk through their space.
- In your discussions, ask how useful the planning element has been for pupils and how, if at all, it helped them to focus their thoughts clearly.

▼ Assessment focus

Pupils can:
- use geometric shapes in a drawing package to create a plan;
- relate their plan to 3-D models;
- talk about their designs and the usefulness of the computer as a planning tool.

Learning objectives ▼

Pupils learn to:
• select an irregular shape using the 'lasso' tool;
• copy and paste the shape into another image to form a montage;
• transpose discussions and ideas into composite images.

ICT resources ▼

Software such as *Granada Colours* (Granada Learning) or similar paint package
Selection of scanned photographs
Scanner
Colour printer

Vocabulary ▼

composition
montage
lasso
superimpose

▼ Introduction

• Look at abstract landscapes by a variety of artists, such as Miró, Magritte, Chagall, and discuss ways in which the artist has created a dream-like effect, using partial reality but changing details.
• Discuss what pupils dream about. Dreams are often our fears and insecurities, and they can also be about things we really want or which make us happy.
• In order to explore this idea on computer, pupils are going to create a landscape by superimposing images, for example a mountain scene, with faces on the mountainside, or a desert landscape with tropical flowers.
• Linking with their hopes and wishes for the future, ask pupils to think about a scene which could portray fame, wealth or being popular amongst one's friends.

▼ Suggested activities

- Pupils research two photographs which they want to use for their project, either from those you have collected or those in a clip art file.
- Pupils open the paint package and import one photograph from which they want to take a part.
- They click on the 'lasso' tool and then draw around the chosen part of the photograph and 'copy' the selected area.
- Then they open a new document and import the second of their chosen photographs.
- Finally, they 'paste' their selected image into the new photograph.
- Pupils are able to move the pasted image before they click elsewhere to deselect it.
- Discuss with pupils the effect they have wanted to produce. What do other groups feel? Are there improvements that could be made? How could this develop by adding other images? Does it have to be photographs or could there be clip art and text? Would symbols help? If so, what?

▼ Assessment focus

Pupils can:
- use the 'lasso' tool to select an irregular shape;
- copy and paste it into a chosen part of another image;
- discuss the intended meaning and think about how they will develop their work;
- relate their own work to that of artists they have studied.

Learning objectives ▼

Pupils learn to:
- use a digital camera to import photographs into the computer;
- develop their awareness of the use of different angles and viewpoints;
- use an image-editing program.

ICT resources ▼

Software such as *Picture It!* (Microsoft), *2paint+* (2simple Educational Software), *Photoshop* or similar image-editing program
Digital camera
Colour printer

Vocabulary ▼

digital
montage
image edit
angle
viewpoint

▼ Introduction

- Discuss with pupils how they might use some of the school buildings as a background for a dreamscape.
- Encourage them to think about changing the angle of a photograph – a part of a roof seen from below, or a shot of a familiar part of the building using a mirror.
- Ask pupils to explore possibilities at playtime, using a piece of card as a viewfinder, and to report back.
- When the weather is wet, ask pupils to look at the reflections of the buildings or of people and to try to describe the mood and effect.
- Explain that some programs on the computer are able to produce similar effects as well, and are called 'image-editing' programs.
- Pupils will use their own images and some of the computer effects to create a montage which provides a setting for a dream.

▼ Suggested activities

- Pupils take photographs in groups with the digital camera, then 'download' the images into a central folder.
- Pupils then open *Picture it!* or a similar package and go to the section on montage.
- They import their photographs to make their montage, resizing, repositioning and rotating their images once on-screen. They can also layer images, and use filters to further change the photograph's appearance.
- Pupils may also add portraits to their montage.
- Discuss finished montage pieces from each group.

▼ Assessment focus

Pupils can:
- take photographs using a digital camera and import them into the computer;
- understand how different angles and viewpoints change the style and mood of the photograph;
- use the montage facility of an image-editing program.

Learning objectives ▼

Pupils:
- study a given artist's work for use of colour and style of brushwork;
- use 'brush' and 'spray' tools to create a specific style;
- talk about why they have used certain techniques which relate to their chosen artist.

ICT resources ▼

Software such as *Granada Colours* (Granada Learning), *Dazzle Plus* (SEMERC) or similar paint package
Colour printer

Vocabulary ▼

brush
spray

▼ Introduction

- Show pupils landscapes by Matisse, Monet and Seurat which use colours in unusual ways.
- Ask pupils to describe to you how the paint has been applied – broad 'dabs' of colour, dots or swirls of colour.
- Encourage pupils to work on these colour mixes and styles in their sketchbooks.
- Tell pupils that you would like them to prepare a signature of one of the artists they have been studying – not a copy of the signature on the painting, but their own design where the shape and style of the letters give a clear idea of the way the artist has painted.

▼ Suggested activities

- Pupils open their paint package, choose the 'brush' tool and right click to change its shape and size.
- Pupils then experiment with the brush to form the first letter of the artist's name.
- Encourage them to think of the shape and style. For example, The 'S' of Seurat might 'float' off in dots of colour at the top and bottom of the letter, or the 'M' of Monet be made to shimmer like his paintings of water.
- They will be able to change the colours to create their own blends by clicking on the palette.
- Discuss finished signatures with pupils. Did they find it easy to 'mix' their own colours to match those of the painting? How does the style of the lettering relate to the artist's work?

▼ Assessment focus

Pupils can:
- create a range of colours using the palette;
- create a style of lettering appropriate to the style of the artist's work;
- use the 'brush' tool in a variety of ways;
- talk about the use of colour and brush style of artists they have studied.

28 Finding Out About Chairs ▼

Learning objectives ▼

Pupils:
- search a large database on the Internet for a given designer's work;
- copy images from the Internet and scan their own chosen images;
- build a sketchbook page combining a computer-generated montage with their own work.

ICT resources ▼

Software such as *Picture It!* (Microsoft) or similar image-editing software
Colour printer
Internet www.designmuseum.org

Vocabulary ▼

Internet
montage
function

▼ Introduction

- Explain to pupils that they are going to search a large database on the computer, using the Internet to find out about particular designers and particular styles of chairs.
- They will then use their skills in montage to create a page (or pages) for their sketchbooks, to which they will add their own ideas and notes.
- Encourage pupils to sort their ideas into those categories for which they will be researching chair design – ceremonial, mass use, comfort, outdoor. Talk about examples of seating in each area.
- Show them the site(s) from the Internet which you have marked as favourites or opened for pupils in advance.

Designmuseum
London by Tower Bridge

Sweet 2000
3D Photography, Nick Knight.
Styling: Jane How.
Animation: Dominic Wright, Createc
© SHOWstudio

About the Design Museum | Exhibitions and Events | Education | Supporting the Design Museum | Hiring the Design Museum | Design at the Design Museum | Digital Design Museum

▼ Suggested activities

- Pupils choose their research area from the home page of the site you have opened.
- According to their level of confidence, you may want to give more specific pointers to pupils in the form of prompts on the board.
- They then copy relevant photographs and paste them into a personal folder for later use, noting each designer's name.
- Pupils also scan images they have found in magazines or from other research on CD-ROM.
- They then arrange their seating as thumbnails in a montage section of their image-editing software, in preparation for the creation of a sketchbook page.
- Finally, they place their printed work onto a larger piece of paper and add notes to the images, plus sketches and ideas of their own, if they choose.
- Discuss the use and importance of the Internet for this type of research, where thousands of images are available to help build up a background of knowledge about this and any other type of design.

▼ Assessment focus

Pupils can:
- search a large database on the Internet and copy illustrations found;
- scan images and import them into image-editing software;
- create a montage of researched images;
- print and add notes and sketches to a montage created on computer.

Learning objectives ▼

Pupils:
- create an outline and style for a journey painting or collage;
- understand more about colour and line in their journeyscape;
- use tools such as that for symmetry to help them to create their journey map.

ICT resources ▼

Software such as *Granada Colours* (Granada Learning) or similar paint package
Colour printer

Vocabulary ▼

symmetry
symbol

▼ Introduction

- Explain that pupils are going to explore a different way of making a landscape which shows a journey and has similarities with maps taken from aeroplanes.
- Show pupils aerial maps and a selection of mazes. Discuss the patterns and lines and the differences in the lines and colours. Look at the shapes of mazes or knot garden designs to give pupils ideas about the shape of their own journey map.
- How might pupils represent a journey to and from school? Do they follow the same route? Would a symmetrical pattern be of use? Which are the interesting parts of the journey? What colours would they choose? How would they colour the outward and return journeys to depict their feelings about the travelling?
- Explain that pupils can explore these areas on computer using their paint program.

▼ Suggested activities

- Pupils open their paint package and explore different ways of making their journey, with shapes for events or things to see and lines of different colours, shapes and sizes for the journey in-between each event or place.
- Pupils can also decide on the shape of their journey. Is it circular, square or diamond-shaped?
- Pupils save their plan and print a copy so that they can use it in the next activity.
- Discuss with pupils why they have chosen a particular shape for their journey. How do pupils depict excitement, fear, danger, and anticipation by their use of colour and shape of line?

▼ Assessment focus

Pupils can:
- use the 'symmetry' tool to create an outline for a journey;
- explore line and colour to add mood to their journey;
- discuss with others their use of shape and line.

30 Symbols for the Journey Painting ▼

Pupils will:
- create an outline and style for a journey painting or collage;
- understand more about colour and line in their journeyscape;
- use the 'symmetry' and other tools to help them to create their journey map.

ICT resources ▼

Software such as *Granada Draw* (Granada Learning) or similar vector drawing package
Colour printer

Vocabulary ▼

symbol
collage
geometric shapes

▼ Introduction

- Explain that pupils are going to explore different symbols they might use to represent events on their journey or places they see.
- Show pupils an atlas that has a key with a range of symbols. Can they see how useful this is on a map?
- Encourage pupils to invent their own symbols.
- Explain that pupils can explore symbols on computer using a drawing program which allows them to make their own shapes and also import clip art to go with the shapes.

▼ Suggested activities

- Pupils open their drawing package and click on the 'shapes' bank. There is a range of shapes available and pupils can follow a simple set of instructions in their manual to change a shape by adding or subtracting curves, arcs of circles, points to a star, for example.
- Pupils explore their shapes. They can use the clip art bank to help as well, creating their own blend of symbols.
- Pupils save their symbols and then look at their copy of the journey outline from the previous activity (see p.56).
- They select and copy each symbol, open their journey outline and paste it into place. They can resize and reposition the symbol *before* they deselect it. Once deselected it is fixed and cannot be moved.
- Discuss with pupils their symbols for the journey. How do they link with the colours and shapes which pupils chose for their connecting lines for the journey? Are there things they would now amend? If so, which things and why?

▼ Assessment focus

Pupils can:
- use the 'shape' tools to create symbols for a journey map;
- blend clip art and geometric shapes to create more developed symbols;
- import symbols to a prepared outline map;
- discuss with others their use of symbols, colour and line.

Learning objectives ▼

Pupils will:
- search a given Internet site for information;
- copy and paste information into image-editing software;
- create sketchbook material on the work of other craftspeople.

ICT resources ▼

Software such as *Picture it!* (Microsoft) or similar image-editing package
Internet www.caa.org.uk
Colour printer

Vocabulary ▼

website
montage

▼ Introduction

- Explain that pupils will use the Internet to research different types of containers, and look at the work of contemporary designers who have exhibited recently at the Contemporary Applied Arts (CAA) in London.
- Pupils will use an image-editing program to arrange their research into a sketchbook page and either add notes on computer or by hand.
- Look at the site's archive before setting the task for pupils. For example, an exhibition from the year 2000 on glass containers, and one of four women working in clay, both of which will help to broaden pupils' thinking about size, shape and uses of containers. One of the four women has made coil containers which are nearly two metres tall.
- Choose similar projects at the time you work, and write down for pupils that you want them to search caa.org.uk, look in the archive section and find either a name or a title of a project specified by you.

Contemporary Applied Arts

2 Percy Street
London W1T 1DD
T 020 7436 2344
F 020 7436 2446

Open Monday to Saturday
10.30am to 5.30pm

Underground Goodge Street
and Tottenham Court Road

(Enlargeable images)

WELCOME   EXHIBITING   NEWS   EDUCATION   BOOKSHOP   ARCHIVE

▼ Suggested activities

- Pupils log on to the Internet and type in the address of the CAA.
- They perform their search as you have requested and right click to copy information ready to paste to their own folders.
- They then open *Picture it!* or similar image-editing software and go to the section on montage. (There is a tutorial to help them to see how this is done if it is the first time they have used the software.)
- Pupils add each image to their montage screen as thumbnails, and then choose how they will arrange them.
- Remind pupils that they may select any image and rotate it, resize it or place it part way behind another image.
- Encourage them to experiment with their screen.
- Pupils then place this page into their sketchbooks and add their own ideas, or add a border to the page to fix any colours or patterns they have seen (they will look further at pattern for decoration in the next activity).
- Discuss ideas the pupils may now have for containers of their own design, and encourage them to say what their starting point is, i.e. which designer has inspired them with ideas.

▼ Assessment focus

Pupils can:
- use the computer to research an Internet site;
- use the montage section of an image-editing program to present their ideas;
- talk about their findings and what ideas the research has given them.

Learning objectives ▼

Pupils learn to:
- search a CD-ROM for visual information;
- copy and paste information into a paint program;
- create linear patterns based on those of another culture.

ICT resources ▼

Software such as *Granada Colours* (Granada Learning) or similar paint package
Corel Clip Art Gallery or similar collection of clip art
Colour printer

Vocabulary ▼

half drop repeat
linear pattern
tile
select an area
edit

▼ Introduction

- Explain that pupils will use their skills in creating tiled patterns to help with their design of a linear pattern to decorate their container.
- Show pupils some patterns from African or Far Eastern ceramics and discuss the repeats, style and shape of the elements used, and how they are applied. Are they painted, scraped or cut into the surface?
- Choose an area for pupils to research. Corel Clip Art Gallery has several excellent sections on African, Chinese, Korean and Japanese designs.
- Explain that in the paint program they will concentrate on the 'tile' and 'tile and half drop' functions.

▼ Suggested activities

- Pupils put the CD-ROM of the clip art selection into the computer and browse to find the areas you suggest.
- They perform their search and as they find illustrations, right click to copy them.
- They then open their paint package and paste an image into a new document.
- Using the 'select an area' tool, pupils select all or part of their image and then go to 'edit' and 'tile' to see what it makes as an overall pattern. They also try 'tile and half drop' to see what their pattern looks like.
- Encourage pupils to experiment with different parts of an image and different selections. They can print in black and white and compare several versions.
- Discuss with pupils how they may apply their patterns to their containers. Will they paint the pattern, etch it or appliqué it in another material?

▼ Assessment focus

Pupils can:
- use the computer to search a CD-ROM;
- use functions of a paint program to explore ideas;
- talk about their findings and what they intend to do with the results of their research.

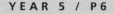

Learning objectives ▼

Pupils learn to:
- group colours into families;
- create effects of light and shade to make 3-D objects on-screen;
- relate their experiments to their still-life compositions.

ICT resources ▼

Software such as *Granada Colours* (Granada Learning) or similar paint package
Colour printer

Vocabulary ▼

spray gun tool
overpaint
colour family

▼ Introduction

- Look at the colour wheel with pupils and study a family of colours placed next to each other, e.g. blue to purple.
- Ask pupils to look at a still life by Monet and to find an object within it which is painted using a family of colours.
- Discuss how shades or tints of the family have been used to produce a 3-D effect for the object.
- Check that pupils understand that a shade is a darker tone of a colour and a tint a paler one.

▼ Suggested activities

- Pupils open their paint package and right click on the 'colour family' symbol, a circle with four colours around it.
- They see a window offering the choices of colour families and choose one set.
- As pupils use either the 'brush' or 'pencil' tool from this point onwards, it will automatically paint in that colour family. The faster they move the brush or pencil, the further apart the colours are.
- Pupils can change one colour in the family by clicking on the colour palette.
- Pupils then draw a circle and use the new brush skill to create a sphere, showing the light source.
- Pupils can also overpaint with the 'spray gun' tool whilst in 'colour family' mode and add more depth to their experimental sphere.
- Discuss other uses of this type of experiment for still life. What other objects might pupils be able to create? Does the tool help to create a richer blend of colour? Is it easy to use?

▼ Assessment focus

Pupils can:
- use the paint program to explore colour families;
- use the tools to create a 3-D effect on screen;
- relate their experiments to their work on still life.

34 Composition ▼

Learning objectives ▼

Pupils learn to:
- group objects with a specific focal point;
- use computer software as a planning tool;
- develop their skills in creating objects in 3-D.

ICT resources ▼

Software such as *Granada Draw* (Granada Learning) or similar drawing package
Colour printer

Vocabulary ▼

intersecting
composition
edit

▼ Introduction

- Explain that pupils will use the computer to explore 3-D objects, and how to place them in an interesting way to create their compositions.
- Look at paintings of still-life groups and ask pupils to count the objects used. They will quickly see that even the simplest composition is made up of an uneven number of objects.
- Ask them to decide on the focal point, the place the eye goes to first, and to try to describe where that place is on the canvas.
- Explain that many artists work to a system where they split the canvas into three equal sections horizontally and vertically and that the places where the lines intersect become the four places where they position an 'important' object.

▼ Suggested activities

- Pupils collect three or five simple objects such as cups, glasses, bottles, salt cellars to place next to the computer.
- They open their drawing package and divide their screen into thirds as you have described.
- They then create their chosen objects in outline geometric shape, based on what they see in front of them.
- They will be able to adjust the curves of the outlines by using the 'edit' tool at the top of the screen.
- Pupils then position their objects in different ways, looking at the intersecting thirds, the places where the lines meet, and at how they can partly overlap their objects to create more interest.
- Encourage pupils to try out more than one grouping and to print their results so they can compare them.
- Pupils keep going back to their objects and repositioning them based on what they have planned on the computer and discuss the different results within their group.

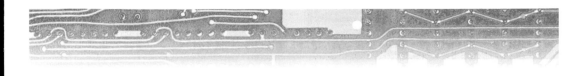

- Once pupils have experimented with the placing of their objects they can start to think about the light source for their composition and to add shading to create a 3-D effect.
- If the light is coming from a window at the left of their composition, then all objects will be affected in the same way and will be lighter on the left than the right.
- Ask pupils to study this carefully, and highlight the action by placing a table lamp at one side of their group of objects so that they can see the effect more clearly.
- Discuss the use of the computer for this planning exercise. Do pupils find that it helps them to create an interesting group? Has it helped with where to shade objects? Could they take the exercise further and add colour using their colour families?

▼ Assessment focus

Pupils can:
- use the computer to aid composition;
- use the 'edit' tool in a drawing program to create the correct shapes for their objects;
- use the 'shading' tools to show the source of light in a composition.

37 Skywalking ▼

Learning objectives ▼

Pupils will:
- develop skills in composition and proportion;
- draw out a geometric pattern from a cityscape;
- develop their understanding of architectural styles from other countries.

ICT resources ▼

Software such as *Granada Colours* (Granada Learning) or similar paint package; *Granada Draw* (Granada Learning) or similar drawing package
Corel Clip Art Gallery or similar collection of clip art, containing photographs of cities around the world
Colour printer

Vocabulary ▼

proportion
composition

▼ Introduction

- Look at a variety of photographs from different countries.
- Supply photographs which illustrate how Western European and American architecture has influenced Africa or the Far East – modern skyscrapers placed next to traditional temples – and discuss with pupils how the architecture itself can show how cultures are merging and developing.
- Explain that pupils will research and find their own photograph of an urban landscape, and use the computer to recreate a skyline without moving the 'pencil' tool from the screen.

▼ Suggested activities

- Pupils browse through the CD-ROM of clip art to find images of city scenes in different styles.
- Pupils print a copy for use in their activity.
- They then open the paint or drawing package and choose the 'freehand pencil' or 'straight line pencil' tool.
- Pupils then take the pencil for a walk, recreating the skyline in one continuous line.
- Encourage pupils to experiment and save each attempt as copy 1, 2, 3, etc. for use in the discussion.
- Discuss with pupils their explorations. How did the first attempt work out? Has their 'eye' for the proportions improved as they made more attempts? Do their 'abstract' outlines highlight differences in architectural styles?

▼ Assessment focus

Pupils can:
- use the computer to search a CD-ROM;
- use functions of a paint program to create abstract, geometric outlines;
- understand more about proportion;
- talk about their activity and relate it to their studies of a variety of urban landscapes.

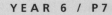

38 Space and Distance ▼

Learning objectives ▼

Pupils will:
- use a digital camera to explore different viewpoints and angles of landscape;
- develop their sense of aerial perspective;
- explore tones and tints of colour and use of proportion in landscape.

ICT resources ▼

Software such as *Granada Colours* (Granada Learning) or similar paint package; *Granada Draw* (Granada Learning) or similar drawing package
Examples of landscape as clip art photographs in Corel Clip Art Gallery or similar
Digital camera
Colour printer

Vocabulary ▼

perspective
aerial
digital camera
clip art size
layering

▼ Introduction

- Look at paintings of landscapes by different artists. Draw out from pupils ideas about how the artist has captured the idea of distance using colour and size.
- Discuss also the composition of the paintings. Where is the focal point? Do pupils remember work on still life where they divided their page into thirds (activity 34, pages 62–63)? Where the lines intersect are 'golden' focal points which will help create a balanced composition.
- Explain that you want pupils to explore three things on computer – use of tints of colour getting paler as the eye moves further away from the foreground, size of buildings getting smaller, and the balance of the composition using the rule of thirds.
- They will create a simple plan of a landscape containing distant hills, two buildings and trees in the foreground.

▼ Suggested activities

- Pupils open their drawing package and divide their screen into thirds horizontally and vertically.
- They first decide on their skyline, and use a gradation of colours to form the background to their landscape.
- They then import clip art of trees and buildings from a clip art collection.
- Encourage pupils to experiment with both the size and position of their objects within the landscape.
- Discuss their landscapes.

▼ Assessment focus

Pupils can:
- use the computer to search a CD-ROM;
- use functions of a drawing program to help them understand more about distance, composition and perspective;
- talk about their activity and relate it to their studies of landscapes.

Learning objectives ▼

Pupils will:
- develop skills in colour and pattern;
- work into a scanned collage;
- isolate parts of computer-generated design for possible borders for headgear.

ICT resources ▼

Software such as *Granada Colours* (Granada Learning) or similar paint package; *Granada Draw* (Granada Learning) or similar drawing package
Colour printer
Scanner

Vocabulary ▼

brush
tint
spray can
select an area

▼ Introduction

- Explain that pupils will use the computer to help develop their understanding of colour and pattern, by adding to a scanned image of a fabric collage.
- Look at a variety of headgear from different countries and for different purposes: ceremonial, religious, festival. The Brazilian carnival in Rio de Janeiro, or its equivalent in England at Notting Hill will be good sources.
- Ask pupils to collect fabrics and pieces of decoration to begin sketchbook studies of colours and textures.

▼ Suggested activities

- Pupils scan their fabric collage into the computer. They look for areas which appear 'flat' and, using a restricted colour palette, work into those areas to add interest.
- Pupils regularly save their work in different versions so that they can compare different effects.
- Encourage pupils to use the range of techniques available: 'brush', 'tint', and 'spray can' tools, dots of colour as well as full areas.
- Pupils then choose areas of their work which may be useful for borders or patterns for their headgear and, using the 'select an area' tool, isolate them in a new document, printing the results for the discussion.
- What did pupils add to their original fabric collage? Did this help to develop their work? Can they see the computer as a useful tool for development of artwork?

▼ Assessment focus

Pupils can:
- use a restricted colour palette;
- work into a scanned collage, using a range of tools in a paint package;
- isolate parts of computer-generated design for possible borders for headgear;
- talk about the use of the computer as an additional tool for generating artwork.

40 Carnival Time ▼

Learning objectives ▼

Pupils learn to:
- use multimedia software to create an animated presentation;
- choose parts of sketchbook and finished items as a part of their presentation;
- add sound to their presentation.

ICT resources ▼

Software such as *HyperStudio 4.0* (Knowledge Adventure inc) or similar package;
Compose World Junior (ESP)
Digital camera
Scanner

Vocabulary ▼

multimedia
animation
montage

This activity relates to activity 39 Get Ahead.

▼ Introduction

- Explain that pupils will use *HyperStudio 4.0* to prepare a presentation of their headgear from the previous activity, which includes detailed background, animated headgear, and sound files composed especially for the presentation.
- In groups, pupils choose from their sketchbooks any interesting parts of their preparation for their designs.

▼ Suggested activities

- Pupils photograph their finished headgear using a digital camera.
- They then scan their chosen parts of sketchbooks, and save to a personal folder.
- Pupils open *HyperStudio 4.0* or a similar package and create a new stack. They choose a background colour first, and then import the scanned images from their sketchbooks to add interest to their background.
- In the 'actions dialogue' box they click on 'animation' and then import their photographs of headgear.
- Pupils draw the pathway they want their animation to take and click 'done'.
- They could also assign the computer to play a sound at the same time.
- Pupils can also assign different methods of changing from one card to the next within their presentation.
- Discuss the presentations with pupils and ask other groups for comments. Does the music help to give an idea of its style and purpose? Has the computer helped in presenting work?

▼ Assessment focus

Pupils can:
- scan a collage into the computer and photograph using a digital camera;
- create a presentation using multimedia software, including animation;
- discuss the appropriateness of their presentation in showing the style of their completed artwork.

Learning objectives ▼

Pupils will:
- use a video recorder to isolate different movement patterns;
- create a series of sketches from the video of the figure in movement;
- talk about how a video machine may be used to study the body in movement.

ICT resources ▼

Learning resources: Digital Video Camcorder

Vocabulary ▼

movement
slow motion
video playback

▼ Introduction

- Ask volunteers to perform a sequence of throwing an object in slow motion.
- Stop the action repeatedly and ask pupils to describe the position of torso, arm and leg.
- Discuss how this might be done using a camera – either a series of stills, or a camcorder to study the movement repeatedly.
- In groups, pupils prepare a sequence to show one of a variety of positions – throwing, walking, running, a sporting activity or a dance sequence.
- Talk about how they will prepare to use the camera – rehearse the sequence so that it is the same each time, discuss what the subject will wear so that the movement can be seen clearly.

▼ Suggested activities

- Pupils film another pupil and look carefully at more than one sequence.
- They 'direct' their model if what they see in the viewfinder is not what they have agreed as a sequence.
- They then put the video into the playback machine and make a 'thumbnail sketch' of the opening position.
- Pupils then move the video forward one or more frames to a second position, linked to the first.
- They add a thumbnail slightly offset to one side of the first so that it 'ghosts' the person moving.
- Pupils carry on to prepare five or six thumbnails.
- Discuss the sketches. Does the process help pupils to understand how the body moves? Who might use this sort of technique? (animation designers)

▼ Assessment focus

Pupils can:
- use a camcorder to capture a movement sequence;
- use a playback machine to capture the movement frame by frame;
- understand more about how the body moves.

42 Animated Action ▼

42 Animated Action ▼

Learning objectives ▼

Pupils will:
- develop their understanding of the human body in movement;
- scan their own figure drawings;
- use a multimedia package to animate a figure.

ICT resources ▼

Software such as *HyperStudio 4.0* (Knowledge Adventure inc) or similar package
Scanner

Vocabulary ▼

movement
animation
frames

▼ Introduction

- Show pupils sequences of movement by artists and photographers such as Muybridge, or the dance photographer Lois Greenfield.
- Ask pupils to look at their own sketches of figures and to choose four which show a sequence, such as the beginning part of a throwing action, where the arm is slowly raised.

▼ Suggested activities

- Pupils scan their sketches into the computer and save them to a folder for retrieval.
- They then open their multimedia package.
- As pupils place their first sketch on to the screen, they choose the 'animation editor' from the menus and specify the pathway they want the animation to take.
- They are given the choice of drawing the pathway to animate the individual figure, or to choose more sketches and animate a sequence.
- They then create their animation of four sketches.
- Pupils may also add backgrounds and other clip art to their screen if they wish, and make the animation live when the first figure is clicked on.
- They save their work for presentation and discussion.
- Discuss with pupils their animations. Does the process help them to understand how the body moves? Who might use this sort of technique? (animation designers) Did they discover that they could change the speed of the animation to make the figure move more quickly or slowly?

▼ Assessment focus

Pupils can:
- scan their own work and save it to a personal folder;
- use a multimedia package to animate a figure in a movement sequence;
- understand more about how the body moves.

Glossary ▼

bookmark/favourites	saves the Internet address of a site to a short cut in the drop down menu of the Internet browser
branching database	a hierarchical database
button/icon	a small image or picture representing a command or function
CD-ROM	Compact Disc Read-Only Memory – an external storage system
cell	a box in a spreadsheet which can hold either data or a formula
change plane	to change from horizontal/vertical to vertical/horizontal
classify	sort into groups of the same or similar items, events, etc.
click select	clicking the mouse
control	in ICT means using software commands to control a device
control box	a device through which the computer controls devices and components
control software	the software used to communicate with the control box/interface
cut and paste	to move words, numbers or images within an application
database	a collection of information held in computer-readable form
datafile	a collection of records in a database
drag	to click on a screen object (e.g. a word or an image) and move it using the mouse pointer
drop	when dragging an object releasing the left mouse button will 'drop' it in its new position
editing	amending and altering data
elasticity	the amount the material will stretch
field	a single heading on a record 'card'
file	data that has been entered and saved with a filename
font	a style of typeface
graphics	in ICT means computer-generated images
hyperlink	links on web pages which are generally underlined and identified by a colour, e.g. blue, which will load up the address of another web page
icon	image on screen which represents a program, file, etc.
import	to bring into a document an image, text, etc. from another source, e.g. a disk file, the Internet, etc.
input	in computer control means whatever gives an instruction, e.g. a switch, sensor, etc.
insert	in ICT means putting a word, graphic, clip art, etc. into a document
invert	to change from positive to negative
lever	a bar which pivots on a fixed point as a mechanical aid
links	areas on a web page or CD-ROM which will take you to another site or section
load	to install a program in memory
logging on	gaining access to a network, local or the Internet
menu	a table of choices
modelling	in ICT means a virtual environment in which ideas can be realised, e.g. making a circuit which lights up, a graphical representation

montage	a collection of images overlaid and designed to convey mood, feeling or for use as part of a sketchbook as a record of a number of ideas
mouse	an input device for selecting objects on the screen
multimedia	combination of text, graphics, sound, video clips, animations, digital photographs, etc.
output	in computer control means a response to an instruction, e.g. lamps, motors, buzzers are all output devices
pivot	the point at which a lever moves up and down, rotates
pointer	the mouse cursor
print	to output text or graphics via a printer
procedures	a list of instructions, within a computer control program, that control a specified event or series of events, e.g. to make a light flash
program	a set of instructions to make a computer perform a task or job
push to break	in computer control this refers to a push button switch that, when pressed, will break the circuit and switch the device off
push to make	in computer control this refers to a push button switch that, when pressed, will complete the circuit and switch the device on
record	one component set of information in a database
robot	a device which can be controlled using a program of instruction
run	to start a program in memory
screen or VDU	output device providing the user with feedback from the computer
search	to make the computer go through all or part of the records in its database to find those that correspond to certain criteria
sensor	a device for sensing changes in the environment
simulation	an imitation of a real-life activity or scenario on the computer
sort	to put records into an order or into groups
spreadsheet	a grid which can hold both data and formulae
thermal	an insulating quality, e.g. materials which keep heat in
URL	Uniform Resource Locator or Internet address
website	a set of web pages belonging to one organisation or person
word bank	a list of words in a file within a word processor or desktop publishing program from which pupils can select and insert into their document

Index ▼